Becoming
God's Community

For no other foundation can any one lay than that which is laid, which is Jesus Christ.
— 1 Corinthians 3:11

Becoming God's Community

John Driver

The Brethren Press
Elgin, Illinois

Evangel Press
Nappanee, Indiana

Faith and Life Press
Newton, Kansas

Mennonite Publishing House
Scottdale, Pennsylvania

Scripture quotations, unless otherwise noted, are from the Revised Standard Version of the Bible, copyrighted 1946, 1952, © 1971, 1973.

A publication of The Foundation Series for Adults

Executive Director: Helmut Harder.

Published by the Brethren in Christ Church, E. Morris Sider, editor; the Church of the Brethren, June A. Miller, editor; the General Conference Mennonite Church, Elizabeth Yoder, editor; and the Mennonite Church, Levi Miller, editor. Cooperative user: the Mennonite Brethren Church, Dennis Becker, editorial representative.

Designers: David Hiebert, Ken Stanley

Script for quotations: Esther Ruth Shisler

Becoming God's Community

4

Contents

Unit B
The Agenda of the People of God

The Sermon on the Mount in Matthew 5 to 7 has been considered as basic teaching material of the Christian community. This unit is a Bible study of this agenda.

Foreword

"But you are a chosen race, a royal priesthood, a holy nation, God's own people, that you may declare the wonderful deeds of him who called you out of darkness into his marvelous light" (1 Pet. 2:9).

People gather into groups, and organize themselves to do things in groups. This practice is as old as the history of civilization. At times such communities of people have a close personal relationship. Sociologists refer to such close-knit groups as a *Gemeinschaft.* At times communities are united by a less personal formal arrangement. The German word, *Gesellschaft,* is sometimes used to refer to such a group. Group life in one form or another is a common practice among us all.

When people gather together, they pursue certain goals or agendas. Sometimes the goals focus on the needs of people. At other times goals focus on things such as money or products. Still at other times the goal might be the recognition of an achievement. The goals or agendas which motivate people to gather into groups can take a variety of forms.

In developing a foundational study for Brethren in Christ, Church of the Brethren, General Conference Mennonite, Mennonite Brethren, and Mennonite Church people, we are talking about such basic human issues as people coming together and doing things together.

However, this book is not simply sociology and history. This book focuses on those distinctives of how a specific people, God's people, came into being—and are still becoming. *Becoming God's Community* is a description of the specific agenda of this community of God, based on the teachings of Jesus found in Matthew 5 to 7. Further, it is candidly focused on the story and understandings of the believers' churches and what are sometimes called the historic peace churches— Brethren, Mennonites, and Quakers.

To focus on this story and agenda today is not to say that we do not also share other stories which are also important. It is to say that this is our understanding of God's gracious working with a people and of what God would have them do. John Driver has written an excellent biblical overview of this story and the agenda. It should help us to place our Christian experience and calling into perspective both from the Bible and from our contemporary life in the church and society.

The writer, John Driver, has given of his best in this book. He has worked with integrity to provide a fresh new look at God's original intent as seen in the Bible. The views are sometimes more radical than we are used to in our daily life. But he attempts to be true to the Scriptures and challenges us to obedience and to dependence on the grace of God.

Becoming God's Community is the first in a series of eight studies in The Foundation Series for Adults. (See the inside back cover of this book for an outline of the entire curriculum.) The aim of this core curriculum is to provide learning materials for adults which reflect those distinctive aspects of the Christian faith which are emphasized in the Anabaptist vision of the people of God. This curriculum is to help examine this vision as it relates to the Bible and to our life of faithfulness in the church today. We hope, by God's grace, that some measure of these aims will be achieved by the congregations using these studies.—Levi Miller, editor.

8

1.
The Roots of Peoplehood

The Book of Genesis announces its content by its title. Its Greek title suggests that it is the biblical story of beginnings. In the first eleven chapters we read of the origins of humankind and the universe. We catch a fleeting glimpse of humanity before the Fall. Genesis tells the story of the evil effects of the Fall, the origins of cultures, and the distribution of peoples.

But more important, Genesis is the story of the beginning of a people—the people of God which live by faith. In fact, the viewpoint of this community's faith, life, and mission give the entire Book of Genesis its meaning. Therefore, the story of God's promise to Abraham recorded in Genesis 12:1-3 is fundamental. The entire book, the introductory section (Gen. 1—11), as well as the stories of the patriarchs (Gen. 12—50), hinges on this key promise.

The biblical story recorded in Genesis 1 to 11 is highly selective in its choice of materials and interprets how God worked with people. Creation and the Fall, followed with humanity's increasing disobedience to God, finally lead to God's gracious intervention in a new creation—the creation of a people.

According to the biblical vision, creation is the starting point of God's saving action. It sets the stage for the unfolding of God's purpose for his people—Israel, first of all, and, in the fullness of time, the Christian church. The whole drama of redemption is based on God's original intention as revealed in a "good" creation.

We see God's intention for all his creation and for humankind, in particular, in the creation story. Peoplehood is certainly not an afterthought—God intended it from the beginning. Genesis reports that it is the basic community formed for man and woman which bears God's image. The man and woman are the basic human "we" of peoplehood who bear the image of God (Gen. 1:26, 27).

In the Fall sin leads to death. But more than the mere loss of physical immortality, sin led to the loss of life in communion with God and his creation. Although death permeates human existence, a promise is given that life will continue (Gen. 3:20) and hope emerges for the future salvation of humanity.

The drama of the Fall is repeated in the story of Cain and Abel, which also ends on a note of hope when Cain receives a visible mark of God's grace (Gen. 4:15, 16). The story of Noah is a symbol of God's mercy which prevails in the midst of judgment. Finally, the story of Babel brings the first section of Genesis to its climax, pointing to the utter futility of humankind's continuing urge to assume roles which belong to God alone. Ironically, fallen humanity's efforts generally carry within themselves the seeds of the very problem which they seek to avoid. Those who attempted to build a city and to make a name for themselves, lest they "be scattered abroad upon the face of the whole earth" (Gen. 11:4) had, in effect, already anticipated their own fate (Gen. 11:8).

All of the preceding stories illustrating humanity's rebellion—the Fall, Cain's evil, and the Flood—conclude with a

Genesis 12:1-4a

"Now the Lord said to Abram, 'Go from your country and your kindred and your father's house to the land that I will show you. And I will make of you a great nation, and I will bless you, and make your name great, so that you will be a blessing. I will bless those who bless you, and him who curses you I will curse; and by you all the families of the earth shall bless themselves.' So Abram went, as the Lord had told him. "

10

note of hope in the redemptive purpose of God. But hope is missing from the Babel story. This notable omission brings us to the end of the early history on a note of judgment. In this climate of hopelessness the biblical narrative takes up the story of the patriarchs as God's word of grace in response to rebellious humanity. By calling Abraham, God creates a new redemptive alternative—a people who bear his name. It is in the life of the people of God that hope is reestablished for fallen creation.

The Call of Abraham

In contrast to humanity which, in its city-tower building enterprise, was turning its back on God, Abraham's response of obedient faith to God's call showed a new alternative—a people who are both blessed by God and a blessing to all humankind.

The text at the beginning of this chapter is pivotal to understanding salvation history and therefore requires some comments.

1. The people of God are God's new creation. In response to a word from God, history begins anew. There is clearly a parallel between the creation narrative and the call of Abraham. Genesis 1 to 11 is the history of a creation which has ended in the hopelessness of godless arrogance. Genesis 12:1 marks the beginning of a new history. In contrast to the treacherous word of the serpent (Gen. 3:1-5) and the confusion of Babel, God's new word is a clear invitation to begin a new history.

God's initiative expressed in the phrase "Now the Lord said" is basic to our understanding of peoplehood. In his farewell message to Israel, Joshua recalled, "Thus says the Lord, the God of Israel. . . . 'I took your father Abraham from beyond the river and led him through all the land of Canaan and made his offspring many' " (Josh. 24:2, 3). The New Testament picks up this tradition when Stephen begins his summary of salvation history with the statement, "The God of glory appeared to our father Abraham, when he was in Mesopotamia, before he lived in Haran, and said to him, 'Depart from your land and from your kindred and go into the land which I show you' " (Acts 7:2, 3). Biblical testimony clearly shows God's initiative.

From the very beginning, God's people have lived in response to the gracious saving action of their Lord. This act of grace distinguishes them from all other peoples, such as the people of Babel whose greatest human enterprise, however sophisticated and powerful, had proved to be a failure.

2. Abraham and Sarah entered a new history with a sharp break from the old. The new history of God's people always begins with repentance, a radical break with the past and a direction in line with the future of God's promise. The call to "go from your country and your kindred and your father's house" (12:1) indicates that Abraham's move was far more than a mere change of geography.

However, the social, economic, and religious aspects of these moves were undoubtedly of greater consequence than the mere geographical move. Abandoning Ur, the ancient world's greatest center of agricultural, industrial, commercial, cultural, and religious development, for the insecure and unknown life of in semi-nomadic Canaan must have required much personal resolve and courage.

The move also involved a fundamental religious change. Biblical writers remind Israel of its background in polytheism (many gods). "Thus says the Lord, the God of Israel, 'Your fathers lived of old beyond the Euphrates . . . and they served other gods' " (Josh. 24:2). In another Jewish document, which comes from the intertestamental period, we read the following description of the origins of Israel. "This people is descended from the Chaldeans. At one time they lived in Mesopotamia, because they would not *follow* the gods of their fathers who lived in Chaldea. For they had left the *way* of their ancestors, and they worshiped the God of heaven, the God they had come to know" (Judith 5:6-8).

In the Bible terms such as "the way," "to follow," and "to walk" generally carry ethical or moral implications. In the case of Abraham, to stop *following* the gods of his ancestors and to abandon their *way* in order to worship the God of heaven was more than a mere change in worship practice.

This call meant moral and spiritual nonconformity which led him to question the ethical basis of his pagan society. To know the God of Israel is to reorder all of one's life in ways which are consistent with his nature. In Abraham's calling we learn that

12

Angela Osiro, a Kenya delegate to Mennonite World Conference in 1978.

13

the people of God live in a way which reflects the kind of God they serve.

3. The people of God owe their identity to God's effective promise, his grace. "And I will make of you a great nation ... and make your name great ... [and] give you this land to possess" (Gen. 12:2; 15:7). Here the contrast between the people of Babel and the people of God is the sharpest. The peoplehood which they struggled so hard to achieve at Babel had eluded them. The name they sought so diligently to preserve was forgotten in failure (Gen. 11:3, 4, 9). On the other hand, peoplehood with a land and posterity and all that "a name" implies is given to Abraham and his descendants as a free gift of God. This is grace.

God's values are very different from those commonly held in human societies. This conviction runs like a scarlet thread throughout the Bible. Those who abandon their country will receive a land. Those who are no people become a great nation. Those who are childless will have posterity. Israel is secure whenever it trusts God, and not when its military preparedness is at its peak. Jesus' saying, reported six times in the Gospels, "whosoever would save his life will lose it, and whoever loses his life for my sake will find it," is a restatement of this fundamental principle. The people of God owe their very life to God's grace and providence.

4. The purpose of peoplehood is to offer hope in the midst of hopelessness. "And I will bless you ... so that you will be a blessing" (Gen. 12:2). God promised Abraham a people, a name, posterity, a land, possessions, and, personally, peace (Gen. 12:2; 15:5, 12-15), so that he and his heirs might be a blessing to all nations. In Abraham and Sarah the ancient curses which fell upon Adam and Eve, the serpent, the land (Gen. 3:14-19), Cain (Gen. 4:11-13), Canaan following the Flood (Gen. 9:25), and Babel (Gen. 11:1-9) are canceled. The blessed Abraham and Sarah and their posterity became symbol, prototype, and instrument of all future blessing. Abraham, at once, receives the divine blessing given to humanity in the beginning (Gen. 1:22-28) and anticipates the messianic blessing to come.

Biblical election is not a right to privilege, but a call to service. Abraham and Sarah and their spiritual descendants

14

are the instruments of universal blessing. Among the feverish activities of Babel and its heirs, the people of God are the only valid alternative of hope.

5. God's people are saved by faith. Biblical faith is trusting obedience in the face of all evidence to the contrary. "So Abraham went as the Lord told him. . . . And he believed the Lord, and he reckoned it to him as righteousness" (Gen. 12:4a; 15:6). Abraham responded in action rather than in words. Much of Christian history has led us to think that faith consists in "believing the unbelievable." However, the life of Abraham teaches us that faith is more a matter of "attempting the impossible" in response to the divine call. Trusting God meant attempting things which seemed to be humanly impossible. In this sense, "it is people of faith who are the sons of Abraham" (Gal. 3:7).

Again, our distance from Abraham distorts our vision and we tend to lose the realism of his situation. To leave the comfort, security, and well-being of Mesopotamia for a semi-nomadic life in an unknown land is not realistic. The possibility of becoming a great nation when one is childless at the age of 75, and one's wife is sterile and apparently beyond the child-bearing age, is not at all clear. Humanly speaking, Sarah quite reasonably followed a socially acceptable custom of the age, to offer her Egyptian slave, Hagar, to her husband for the purpose of having an heir. But this was not God's way (Gen. 17:21).

To live against the current and to resist shortcuts to obedience, even though they might be socially acceptable, must have involved costly decisions and been the occasion for many anxious moments. But, to trust God meant to obey him. Abraham's faith determined, in the long run, his conduct.

Abraham is a classic example of biblical faith. To believe God's promises is to risk everything, humanly speaking. For precisely this reason, the only alternative open to this kind of trust is obedience. James reminds us that "faith without works is dead." Biblical faith means obedience. To believe is to commit oneself to act. Biblical truth is practiced truth (1 Jn. 1:6).

6. Although Abraham certainly lived in anticipation of the land of God's promise, real life-sustaining land, the writer of

Hebrews offers a theological explanation of Abraham's obedience. "For he looked forward to the city which has foundations, whose builder and maker is God" (Heb. 11:10). This New Testament statement about the nature of the people of God is profound and daring. The writer implies that Ur of the Chaldeans lacked a foundation. As we have already noted, among all the cities of the ancient Near East, Ur appeared to be the most solidly based. It was the prime expression of human intelligence and industry. But according to the biblical evaluation, human efforts and ingenuity had miscarried in the construction of its civilization.

Negatively, Ur was characterized by the violence and hopelessness of the old history. Human efforts had become corrupted. God's call to Abraham to leave the city was, implicitly, divine judgment against its creators. In the biblical view the material part of economic development is not a morally neutral matter. The prophets echo the concern for justice in human creation already implied in Abraham's abandonment of Ur.

Hear this, you heads of the house of Jacob
and rulers of the house of Israel,
who abhor justice
and pervert all equity,
who build Zion with blood
and Jerusalem with wrong. . . .
Zion shall be plowed as a field;
Jerusalem shall become a heap of ruins
(Micah 3:9, 10, 12).

Positively, the Hebrews text tells us that sojourning "in the land of promise as in a foreign land" and "living in tents" in the light of the expected fulfillment of God's promise is the way to look forward "to the city . . . whose builder and maker is God" (Heb. 11:10). In the life of Abraham the future to which God called him determined the values by which he lived in the present.

This passage also contains an authoritative statement about value scales. What God builds with the materials and the means of His own choosing is, in reality, well founded. Only the city of God, built according to His values, will have a future. The people of God, who dare to live by faith, are the true children of Abraham in whom God's promises are fulfilled.

It is of no avail
to talk of the church in general,
the church in the abstract,
unless the concrete
particular local church
which the people attend
can become
a center of light and leading,
of inspiration and guidance,
for its specific community.

— Rufus M. Jones

7. Finally, the texts of Abraham's call show the humanly insecure and precarious beginnings of God's people. The call meant leaving behind the traditional sources of security (Gen. 12:1). Israel's insecure beginnings are the other side of the coin of God's gracious choosing. God's people must never forget that their weakness is the occasion of God's power and their poverty and precariousness is the opportunity for God's love (Deut. 7:6b-8a).

In a pagan environment, anxiously concerned about its own survival, God's people are those who, by definition, live by faith. Their life is a pilgrimage which, when viewed from a purely human view, appears to be insecure. But, in reality, it rests on the sure foundation of God's faithfulness. Throughout history, God's people have constantly been tempted to place their trust in their own wealth and power to secure their future. Therefore the sons and daughters of Abraham must always recall their origins and confess their absolute dependence on God's grace and providence for their survival.

The Children of Abraham

The character of Abraham's faith continues in other stories of his life. That Abraham made the journey to sacrifice Isaac, the child of promise, is evidence of his willingness to fully trust God. Abraham again affirms the biblical truth that one finds life in losing it. Abraham's self-giving spirit stands out in his relationship to Lot. In contrast to Lot's selfish choice of the best land, Abraham is not only content with the poorest, but courageously intervenes to rescue Lot when he is in danger.

Genesis also includes a brief description of the earliest of Sarah and Abraham's children. Isaac, the child of promise, is a peaceable person whose gentle character makes him an apt symbol of covenant values. He depends not so much on his own human effort for his well-being, as he does on the faithfulness of God who has committed himself to support his gracious design for human life.

Jacob illustrates God's interest in those without rights, a basic principle in the life of God's people. In choosing the younger of Isaac's two sons, God shows that his election does not rest on human values or merit. In the end it is not Jacob the supplanter who prevails by his own cleverness. Rather, Israel, transformed by God's blessing, becomes the ancestor of God's people.

Finally, Joseph, the instrument of God's gracious care for his people, provides the bridge between the Genesis story and the experience of the Exodus and Sinai. But that story needs another chapter.

Conclusion

Genesis begins with the story of the Creation and the Fall and culminates in a new beginning with Abraham and Sarah. In the creation of a people, God clearly provides a word of grace to a rebellious humanity. We have noted seven characteristics of that call and creation of God's people. The people of God in both the old and new covenant have identified themselves with Abraham and Sarah, persons of faith. In this story the people of God find their roots.

2.
Growing into Peoplehood

Israel's sense of identity was rooted in the mighty saving acts of God. The two most important were the liberation from bondage in Egypt and the giving of the covenant at Sinai. These two events were the primary sources of Israel's knowledge of God, as they continually recounted in their confessional statements and worship.

The reality and meaning of Israel's peoplehood were anchored in these important events. At times of unfaithfulness, the people of God are called to repentance through appeals to return to their roots in the Exodus and the covenant given at Sinai. Prophet after prophet reminded the Israelites that they owed their very being to God's gracious saving action in calling them out of Egypt and leading them through the wilderness.

After the new covenant is established, God's people become a "new humanity" with God's law written "upon their hearts." Still the Exodus continues as a standard for their understanding of salvation. Like the call of Abraham, the Exodus and Sinai events are pivotal in salvation history. Israel emerges from these experiences with a clear sense of identity as God's people.

Israel Becomes a People in Egypt

Even though the Exodus and the Sinai experiences were

decisive in forming Israel as the people of God, we must remember that in a very real sense Israel had already become a people during the sojourn in Egypt. The family of Jacob became a people even before the oppression began (Ex. 1:7). In its confession of faith Israel continually recalled that their fathers were "few in number" when they went into Egypt as sojourners, but in Egypt they "became a nation, great, mighty and populous" (Deut. 26:5).

These passages, and their contexts, also reflect on the biblical meaning of nationhood. According to the biblical vision, even a band of oppressed and landless aliens are a nation, inasmuch as they receive Yahweh's promises. They are already God's chosen people. Even though they find themselves in bondage in Egypt, Israel is a people who worship the true God. And their groaning in affliction is the occasion for God to remember "his covenant with Abraham, with Isaac, and with Jacob" (Ex. 2:23-25).

It is sometimes suggested that the Exodus shows God's saving activity in all times and places. Therefore God's people should tell the "Pharaohs" of this world, "Let my people go." It is further argued that just as the Exodus came before Mt. Sinai, so political liberation must come before real peoplehood. One can wholeheartedly agree that oppressing the weak at the hands of the strong is a glaring evil committed against the Creator, as well as the creature. Although such sinful oppression in any form must be rejected by God's people, the Bible clearly shows that the Exodus occurred because Israel was *already* God's people.

Peoplehood does not depend on the fulfillment of prior social, economic, or political conditions, but on divine calling and human response of obedience. Peoplehood happened before the Exodus, not because of it. The faith and life of the people of God in Goshen made the Exodus and Sinai experiences possible. In Goshen the people affirmed their identity as the "descendants of Israel" (Ex. 1) by recalling the stories of their forebears and by crying out to God who had appeared to them. Moses owed his very life to midwives who "feared God" (Ex. 1:17) and to parents who acted out of trust in the God of the Hebrews. Sinai and the covenant come after the Exodus in time. But the moral motivation and the community's

21

Do we sometimes wait on God, and so that's all that we get done?

relationship with God were already established. The Exodus is a part of God's response to his worshiping community and his ongoing communion with his people (Ex. 8:2, 20, 26f).

Clearly, from the Exodus story, nationhood, or peoplehood in the biblical understanding, does not grow out of the experience of political liberation, nor out of mere ethnic solidarity. Rather, it happens because of God's grace with a people who respond in obedient faith and worship. In the history of salvation such a community is the place for really radical spiritual, social, and economic changes.

God Liberates His People

The way Israel was freed from bondage in Egypt gives a basic insight into the nature of God's people. Exodus 2:11-15 describes briefly Moses' approach to the problem of oppression. Moses was like most revolutionaries throughout history. Concerned by the injustices suffered by his people, he took justice into his own hands. He killed the oppressor.

One cannot help noticing the contrast between Moses' early fervor on behalf of his oppressed brothers and sisters and the sober statement of God's concern which follows: "And the people of Israel groaned under their bondage, and cried out for help, and their cry under bondage came up to God. And God heard their groaning, and God remembered his covenant with Abraham, with Isaac, and with Jacob" (Ex. 2:23b-25).

At this point the Lord appeared to Moses in the desert say-

Exodus 19:3-6

And Moses went up to God, and the Lord called to him out of the mountain, saying, "Thus you shall say to the house of Jacob, and tell the people of Israel: You have seen what I did to the Egyptians, and how I bore you on eagles' wings and brought you to myself. Now therefore, if you will obey my voice and keep my covenant, you shall be my own possession among all peoples; for all the earth is mine, and you shall be to me a kingdom of priests and a holy nation. These are the words which you shall speak to the children of Israel."

22

ing, "I have seen the affliction of my people who are in Egypt. . . . And I have seen the oppression with which the Egyptians oppress them. Come, I will send you to Pharaoh that you may bring forth my people, the sons of Israel, out of Egypt" (Ex. 3:7, 9, 10). Apparently only a long desert sojourn under the teaching of God would mold the young rebel into a leader capable of understanding the mind of God.

The biblical story reports Israel's liberation from Egypt as a confrontation between the God of Israel and Pharaoh and the gods of the Egyptians. "And you shall say to Pharaoh, 'Thus says the Lord, Israel is my first-born son, and I say to you, "Let my son go that he may serve me"; if you refuse to let him go, behold, I will slay your first-born son' " (Ex. 4:22, 23). The real contest is the conflict between Pharaoh and the God of Israel who had sent Moses. More than Israel's freedom is at stake. It is a question of who controls history: Yahweh, Lord of his en-slaved people, or Pharaoh, the incarnation of the sun-god and master of Egypt.

This struggle theme between God and Pharaoh is repeated over and over in the story. It is set forth in Moses' charge, "The Lord, the God of the Hebrews, sent me to you, saying, 'Let *my* people go, that they may serve *me* in the wilderness; and be-hold *you* have not obeyed' " (Ex. 7:16). In the narrative which follows, this theme is constantly reiterated. "Let *my* people go that they may serve *me* . . . behold, I will plague all *your* country with frogs" (Ex. 8:1d-2). "Let *my* people go, that they may serve *me* . . . behold, I will send swarms of flies on *you* and *your* servants, and *your* people, and into *your* houses" (Ex. 8:20d-21). This contrast is explicitly repeated in the verses which follow (Ex. 9:13-15; 10:3, 4).

The description of the plagues as "signs and wonders" is another motif that repeats in this story (Ex. 4:8, 17, 28, 30; 7:3; 8:23; 10:1, 2). For Israel these wonders and mighty works were signs of their redemption. For Egypt they were signs of judg-ment. "I am the Lord, and I will bring you out from under the burdens of the Egyptians, and I will deliver you from their bon-dage, and I will redeem you with an outstretched arm and with great acts of judgment" (Ex. 6:6; cf. 7:4, 5). God's judgment upon Pharaoh and Egypt's "hardness of heart" and God's re-demptive acts in the midst of His "believing" people are the

The late J. A. Toews, Mennonite Brethren historian and church leader, and Henry H. Dick, pastor of the Reedley (California) Mennonite Brethren Church.

two sides of the coin of God's activity in salvation history. These signs and wonders live on as they are retold in the worship of God's people (Ex. 10:1, 2; Deut. 26:8; 29:3).

The climax of this confrontation between the God of Israel and the powers which ruled Egypt is found in the events of Passover. For that reason the salvation of God's people in the Exodus is commemorated in the "sacrifice of the Lord's passover" (Ex. 12:27). The redeeming grace of God, celebrated in worship, will culminate in the appearing of the "Lamb of God, who takes away the sin of the world!" The life and death and resurrection of God's Messiah will fulfill the ancient Passover feast (Jn. 1:29; 2:23). The Apostle Paul said clearly, "For Christ, our paschal lamb, has been sacrificed" (1 Cor. 5:7b).

The Exodus is God's alternative to Moses' single-handed attempt to free his suffering people from their Egyptian taskmasters. The liberation of God's people meant literally "going out." The plagues and death in Egypt and the destruction in the sea happened because the hardness of Pharaoh's heart would not permit the Exodus to be peaceful. Pharaoh and his taskmasters were not destroyed by the violence of Israel or its leaders, but by the presence of this "different" kind of community. The people of God, provoked Pharaoh to overreach himself, to harden his heart.

One gets the impression that Israel's Exodus is similar to Abraham's withdrawal from the security of Ur of the Chaldeans into the insecurity of God's promise of a name, posterity, and a land. To be sure, some in the "mixed multitude" longed for the security they left behind in Egypt (Ex. 14:10-12). But the Bible indicates that these did not reflect the true spirit of God's people. God's community is called to disassociate from all of their Urs and Egypts with their structures of security and to orient their lives in the hope of "the salvation of the Lord, which he will work" (Ex. 14:13).

God's Mighty Saving Acts

The recital of the mighty saving acts of God is a dominant theme in Exodus and Deuteronomy. The terms which recur in this recital reflect the nature of God's saving activity. God has taken the initiative to save his people. "To bring them out" is a

Jesus did not bring to faith
any new theories about the being
peoplehood and a new way of liv
of such a group is itself a deep
was such a threat that he had
group is not only by its exist
scene; if it lives faithfully, it is
social change.

refrain which is echoed throughout the text. The expression and its variations appears 55 times in Exodus and Deuteronomy.

One of the most attractive figures of speech is found in Exodus 19:4-6. The image of being borne on eagles' wings is further enriched in Moses' song, "Like an eagle that stirs up its nest, that flutters over its young, spreading out its pinions, the Lord alone did lead him" (Deut. 32:11, 12a). The figure highlights the marvelous power of God's saving acts and underscores the weak and insecure nature of Israel's condition. Apparently the eagle taught its young to fly by tossing them out of the nest, and then swooping down and allowing the young bird to alight on its mother's wings. This bird figure vividly shows God's dealings with his people. God bears his people from the "insecurity" of Egypt and its false values to the "security" of the Promised Land, via Sinai and the wilderness.

Another repeated expression in these passages to describe the saving activity of Yahweh notes that God has liberated his

ful Israel any corrected ritual or
of God. He brought them a new
ing together. The very existence
social change. Its very presence
to be crucified. But such a
ence a novelty on the social
also the most powerful tool of
— John H. Yoder

people "by a mighty hand" and "an outstretched arm." This is a Hebrew way of emphasizing the great power by which Israel has been freed from bondage in Egypt. This is a confession that God's power is seen most clearly in the ways in which he saves his people. The power of Israel's God is most manifest in the "coming out" (Exodus) of Egypt to the life of Sinai and the wilderness.

The answer to the rhetorical question "Has any god ever attempted to go and take a nation for himself from the midst of another nation, by trials, by signs, by wonders, and by war, by a mighty hand and an outstretched arm?" (Deut. 4:34) is obviously "no." God's might is shown in his saving acts while his judgments appear as the reverse side of the coin. This helps us to understand why the people of the new covenant see in the cross of Christ's vicarious suffering the "power" of God for salvation. The cross is also the stone of stumbling whereby the unbelief and disobedience of rebellious humankind is judged.

The people who arrived at Sinai were more than a mere

"mixed multitude" of ex-slaves fleeing from their Egyptian taskmasters. They were God's redeemed people, saved by his mighty acts and the object of his steadfast love.

A Covenant of Grace and Law

The peoplehood of Israel is firmly based on the merciful calling of God. Israel was reminded that "the Lord your God has chosen you to be a people for his own possession, out of all the peoples that are on the face of the earth" (Deut. 7:6). Clearly, this election (choosing) did not respond to any inherent goodness or merit to be found in Israel. To the contrary, Israel's election is another example of God's choosing the weak, the poor, and the least, from a human view, to fulfill his purposes. "It was not because you were more in number than any other people that the Lord set his love upon you and chose you, for you were the fewest of all peoples" (Deut. 7:7). It was "not because of your righteousness or the uprightness of your heart" (Deut. 9:5a).

The mystery of divine election lies beyond the range of strictly human logic. Israel's election is rooted in God's love and his faithfulness. "It is because the Lord loves you, and is keeping the oath which he swore to your fathers, that the Lord has brought you out with a mighty hand, and redeemed you from the house of bondage" (Deut. 7:8). The secret of Israel's being is Yahweh, "the faithful God who keeps covenant and steadfast love" (Deut. 7:9).

In ancient Israel there were two distinct forms of covenant: 1) parity, or bilateral, and 2) suzerainty, or unilateral treaties. A parity treaty was one in which the two parties were equals, at least insofar as the treaty was concerned. It was an agreement, a promise, or commitment for mutual benefit or support.

On the other hand, the suzerainty treaty is established unilaterally. One party of the covenant is more powerful than the other party and the treaty is granted largely out of benevolent interests. Strong kings made covenants of this type with their subjects, motivated by kindness and common interests.

The covenant which God established with his people at Sinai is described in the language and forms of the second of these ancient covenant types. God offers his covenant to Israel. The conditions of God's covenant do not respond to his

Burton Buller, a Mennonite cinematographer from Nebraska.

own self-interests, since he needs no subjects to defend him or render services. To the contrary, God's covenant expresses his intention for the well-being of his community and the best interests of his people. The covenant reflects God's love for his people.

This covenant begins with God's acts of grace, "I am the Lord your God, who brought you out of the land of Egypt . . ." (Ex. 20:1). God assumes responsibility for it. Nevertheless, it is by no means forced upon his people. The covenant at Sinai was spontaneously accepted by Israel. "All the people answered together and said, 'All that the Lord has spoken we will do' " (Ex. 19:8).

At Sinai Israel *formally* came together as the people of God, whose life is characterized by the law of God. This coming together of the people of God as a community whose life is governed by God is part of the meaning of liberation. Sometimes the Exodus is considered the "gospel" of grace which introduces God's law. However, a biblical understanding would not always separate these two aspects of God. God's people are a community of grace *and* law. Liberation is *from* bondage and *for* covenant community. In the Bible the *what for* of covenant community appears to be just as important as the *what from* of liberation from bondage. The biblical message is that in reality *both* are good news. Both are gospel. Grace is the context of God's law.

Covenant Worship

Not only does God's community emphasize grace and law. Much attention is also given to worship practices (Ex. 25—31; 35—40; Lev. 1—10; 16—26; *et al.*). Lengthy passages describe the role of the ark of the covenant, the tabernacle, the establishment of a special priesthood, and a system of sacrifices. Surely we have here little more than a formal outline of what must have been meaningful and exciting worship celebrated in prayer, praise, and sacred dance among God's people.

Both the ark of the covenant and the tabernacle in which it was housed were special signs of the continuing presence of God with his people. The ark contained the tables of God's covenant law (Ex. 25:16, 21; Deut. 10:5) and was a constant reminder of God's intention to relate to his people.

The tabernacle, built of materials voluntarily contributed by the people, similarly showed the presence of God among his people. "The door of the tent of meeting" became the place where God met with and spoke to his people (Ex. 29:42, 43). The tabernacle and the ark represented God's presence and his righteousness. The tabernacle became the place where repentance was experienced and relationships were restored. Of special significance among the various sacrifices was the "Day of Atonement" (Lev. 16), in which God's people found their ultimate fulfillment in the unique sacrifice of Jesus Christ (Heb. 9:6-14).

The writers of the New Testament saw the tabernacle as the place of God's presence among his people, as fulfilled in Jesus. "For in him all the fulness of God was pleased to dwell" and "the Word ... dwelt [i.e., tabernacled] among us" (Col. 1:19; cf. 2:9; Jn. 1:14). The tabernacle showed the meaning of the incarnation wherein God continues to "tabernacle" among his people. The tabernacle also pointed to its heavenly fulfillment and the dwelling of God with people, "the holy city, the new Jerusalem, coming down out of heaven from God" (Heb. 8:1-5; 9:11, 24; Rev. 21:2).

Conclusion

The sons of Abraham and Jacob were, in a limited sense, a people when they went into Egypt as sojourners (Is. 52:4). In a fuller sense Israel grew into peoplehood in Egypt. Liberated from Egyptian bondage by the mighty saving acts of Yahweh, this redeemed people became a covenant community of Sinai. The Ten Commandments describe the relationships with God, as well as showing the life of God's people. The tabernacle, a part of worship, showed God's presence with his people finding its fuller meaning in Jesus living among us. Under the new covenant, Christ himself is both the Passover Lamb, as well as the "new Moses." He will deliver the people of God from bondage, will mediate God's "new law," will shepherd them in their wilderness experience of adversity, and will finally lead them into the promised land of God's kingdom.

3.
Preparing for the True Vine

The first five books of the Old Testament come to a close with Moses seeing the land of promise from a distance (Deut. 34). The figure of Moses straining to catch a vision of God's future for his people is a prime example of the Old Testament story of the pilgrimage of God's people. They looked to the future.

The story is a mixed record of human faithlessness and God's faithfulness. Delivering Israel out of Egypt was an act which God accomplished with his mighty arm in the Exodus. However, taking the "spirit of Egypt" out of Israel was a process which continued throughout the rest of the Old Testament period. At times major sectors of the people are on the brink of apostasy. At other times signs of hope appear in the form of spiritual, moral, and worship renewal. But these are insufficient to stave off judgment, and God's people suffer two major exiles at the hands of pagan powers.

But even in the midst of ruin the Old Testament closes with the prophets peering into the future, which the God of the covenant has promised to his people. Zechariah calls on God's people to "sing and rejoice ... for lo, I come and I will dwell in the midst of you.... And many nations shall join themselves to the Lord in that day, and shall be my people" (Zech. 2:10, 11).

Deut 34: 4   covenant renewed

The Switch to the Monarchy

Following the distribution of the land among the families of Israel, the Book of Joshua comes to a close with the renewal of the Mosaic covenant at Shechem. Two things stand out in this passage. The first is the strong initiative God takes on behalf of his people. The personal pronoun "I," referring to God, appears eighteen times in eleven verses. God called Abraham; God liberated Israel from Egyptian bondage; and God gave them Canaan. Second, although this covenant was the gift of Yahweh to his people, they could freely choose to make it theirs, commiting themselves to obedience (24:15, 22). (This was apparently unique in ancient Near Eastern covenant treaties of this type.) Some believe that a covenant renewal rite may have become an annual event in Israel.

The transition from peoplehood under the rule of God with the charismatic leadership (as seen in Judges and the prophets) to kingship was a change of far-reaching consequences. The biblical texts are not fully unanimous in their evaluation of the theological and ethical implications of kingship. (Compare, for example, 1 Sam. 8; 10:17-24; 12; Deut. 17:14-20 with 1 Sam. 9:1-10; 16.) However, clearly kingship, as it was practiced among "the nations," was considered to be a rejection of God's provident rule over his people.

Israel's request for a king was considered a step of unfaith. A certain pathos is found in the repeated phrase, "appoint for us a king to govern us like all the nations . . . that we also may be like all the nations" (1 Sam. 8:5, 20). The pathos is particularly striking because the very reason for Israel's existence is based on its uniqueness, precisely in order to be a blessing to the nations. The people's request for a king is seen as outright rejection of Samuel's leadership, as well as God's provident rule (1 Sam. 8:7). And even when it came, kingship in Israel was to be different (Deut. 17:14-20).

King David illustrates something of the pathos and contradiction of kingship in Israel. His checkered career is a mixture of virtue and human weakness. He is described as "a man after Yahweh's own heart," but the bloody violence of his reign disqualifies him as builder of a temple to Yahweh. His

pathos: an element in experience 33
evoking pity or compassion

questioned loyalty to friends and his regard for the life of the "Lord's anointed" stand in stark contrast to his treachery toward Uriah the Hittite. Possibly David's census laid the groundwork for later taxation and military conscription (2 Sam. 24) and the forced labor of Solomon's reign may actually have begun under David (2 Sam. 20:24).

On the other hand, David's readiness to repent of his sins are obvious signs of God's grace with him. David, rather than Saul, establishes the kingdom, is the object of God's covenant, and becomes the ideal in Israel's messianic expectations. One would come to deliver his people from their enemies and sit upon the throne of David forever. (See Lk. 1:32, 33, 69-71.)

Nevertheless, the history of the monarchy is a sad story. In fact, Solomon's reign was a prime example of what a king should *not* do. In asking for a king "like the nations" God's people had, in reality, pronounced judgment on themselves. In effect, they had become like the nations around them. The kings' reigns are told and evaluated in negative terms.

Only the reformers Hezekiah and Josiah receive anything like approval. Just as Samuel had warned, the kings of God's people became warlords who used their subjects for military purposes and taxed them almost beyond their endurance to support royal programs. They became oppressors more often than shepherds (1 Sam. 8:10-18). Israel, and later Judah, were swept into exile and the only hope for God's people lay beyond judgment. The violence and oppression God's people had experienced before the Exodus returned in new forms under the monarchy. The peace and justice which the Sinai

Isaiah 11:6
The wolf shall dwell with the lamb,
and the leopard shall lie down
with the kid,
and the calf and the lion and the
fatling together,
and a little child shall lead them.

covenant assured God's people were broken by human greed and selfish power grabbing. We will explore these problems and God's solutions.

God's People Survive by His Providence

1. First, in regards to violence and oppression, we earlier noted that Israel's very life was a gift of God. For both their being and their survival God's people needed only to trust in the Lord. This fact is clearly summarized in Joshua 24:1-27. The call of Abraham was the result of God's grace and love (Josh. 24:3). The Exodus from Egyptian slavery was a saving act of God who delivered his people (24:6, 7). The "conquest" of Canaan was another gift of God to his people (24:12, 13). In this evaluation of events Joshua was anticipating by more than half a millennium the prophet Zechariah, "not by might, nor by power, but by my Spirit, says the Lord of hosts" (Zech. 4:6).

In spite of Israel having chosen to become like other nations with kingship and warfare, it is noteworthy that there are many examples in Israel's history where they trusted in God for their survival rather than in their own military might. For example, Judges 7 describes how the Midianite forces were put to flight by Gideon and a band of 300 men armed with trumpets, empty jars, and lighted torches because Yahweh sowed panic among the enemy.

In 2 Kings 6:8-12 Elisha is credited with a victory over the Syrians through his words of prophecy rather than armed might. On another occasion, Syrian armies lifted their siege of Samaria and fled in disarray because "the Lord had made the army of the Syrians hear the sound of chariots and ... of a great army" (2 Kings 6:24—7:20). During the reign of Hezekiah, Sennacherib laid waste a number of cities and besieged Jerusalem. However, Isaiah invited Hezekiah to trust God for deliverance, assuring him that Sennacherib would not enter the city. The military preparedness of Hezekiah did not finally break the Assyrian siege, but God's intervention did. When many in his army mysteriously died, Sennacherib withdrew (2 Kings 19; Is. 36, 37).

On other occasions the armies of Israel used weapons, as well as "trusting in Yahweh" for deliverance. But in their theological interpretation of *all* of Israel's victories (with or without the use of arms) the biblical writers are convinced that deliverance is from God. The God of Israel can be trusted for the survival, as well as the existence of his people.

2. God's answer to social injustice and economic oppression were the provisions in the Sinai covenant. This covenant insured just relationships within his community. The sabbatical and jubilee provisions were especially clear indicators of God's will for the common life of his people.

According to these provisions the land was to be left fallow every seventh year, not merely for ecological reasons, but to continually remember that the earth and its resources are the Lord's. They are given to his people so that all, the poor in particular, may have food to eat (Ex. 23:10, 11).

Indebtedness was also to be forgiven every seven years. The reason was that "the Lord's release has been proclaimed" (Deut. 15:2). Indebtedness is forgiven among the people of God because Yahweh is a forgiving God.

Indentured slaves among the Israelites who have been forced to sell their services to their brethren because of poverty were to be released after seven years. The reason for this was that God has redeemed Israel itself from slavery (Deut. 15:12-18).

And finally, every 49 years family inheritances which had been lost due to economic reversals were to be returned to the original families or to their descendants (Lev. 25:8-31). This provision was because the earth is the Lord's and everyone, from the king to the most lowly, was a son of the loving God and servant of the one and only Lord, Yahweh.

Israel failed miserably in putting these and other provisions into practice. The crying need for social justice in Israel is found on practically every page of the writings on the monarchy and the great prophets of the eighth and seventh centuries BC. In fact, they believed that the exile had come upon God's people as punishment for their refusal to observe sabbatical provisions (Jer. 34:8-22; 2 Chron. 36:21). When God's provisions for governing the distribution of the land and insuring liberty were disregarded, the people found themselves in exile, deprived of both land and liberty.

The prophets who contributed most to Israel's survival as

Takio Tanase, a Mennonite Bible teacher of Obihiro, Japan.

the people of God by pointing to a hope beyond judgment wove the fabric of that hope out of these two vital threads: 1) their nonviolent dependence on God for both existence and survival and 2) the covenant expression of social relationships as highlighted in the sabbatical and jubilee provisions. Isaiah and Micah shared a vision of the future messianic reign characterized by peace (Is. 2:2-4; 9:2-6; 11:1-9; Mic. 4:1-4) and the jubilee announcement of the "year of the Lord's favor" (Is. 61:2). Precisely these two strands were grasped by Jesus to identify his messianic mission.

Hope Beyond Judgment

By the eighth century BC Judah had become the victim of a national theology which was little more than a tool in the hands of the privileged and powerful to maintain the religious and social status quo. In this situation Isaiah and a younger prophet Micah called on leaders and people alike to radical obedience and renewal. In the face of the national disaster, they painted a picture of hope for the future.

Social disintegration and economic exploitation, with the accompaning forms of moral corruption, had reached critical proportions. Religious and civil leaders themselves were guilty of injustice and violence (Mic. 2:1, 2; 3:9-11). The great landholders treacherously dispossessed the poor (Is. 3:13-15; 5:7, 8) who had been victimized by corrupted judges (Is. 1:21-23; 5:23; 10:1-4; Mic. 3:1-3). Meanwhile the rich lived in luxury, unconcerned for the misery of the poor (Is. 3:16; 5:11, 12). Official religion had little to say about these injustices among God's people. Supported by the state, and devoted to defend national interests, this religion had sold its right to criticize evil (Mic. 2:11). In fact, its elaborate, well-financed worship system communicated the false idea that Yahweh's demands could be satisfied by ceremony (Is. 1:10-17).

The Sinai covenant, which celebrated God's great saving acts in behalf of his people and outlined the nature of their relationships, had originally served as a basis for the faith and life of Israel. However, these ancient patterns had progressively fallen into disuse. Instead of being the God who frees the slaves, who is concerned for the sojourner, the orphan, the widow, and the poor, Yahweh had become a sort of national guardian committed to assuring Judah's survival. In return for careful worship practices, Yahweh was expected to pour out his blessing and protection upon the nation *as it was* (Is. 1:10-20).

But there can be no salvation without righteousness. In this sense, the judgment of God upon his people was to save them. For Isaiah and Micah, God's promises would be fulfilled in One who would come to redeem Israel and establish divine rule on earth. The prophets were sure that God was in control of the events of history, even in times of national disaster. God's kingly rule of peace over all nations was sure.

The prophets formulated the classic expression of hope in the ruler from David's line. On this ruler all the gifts of God's grace would rest and in him redemption and divine rule would finally be realized (Is. 9:2-7; 11:1-9; Mic. 5:2-4). Throughout history this messianic vision has been basic to God's people's self-understanding.

God's People of the Messianic Era

Isaiah 11:1-9 offers a number of characteristics of the messianic future which lies beyond judgment. This vision is prominent among the prophets (Is. 2:2-4; 9:1-6; Mic. 4:1-4; 5:2-4; Jer. 23:5, 6). The promises of God offer hope for the future. It would be a new branch, "a shoot from the stump of Jesse, and a branch . . . out of his roots" (Is. 11:1).

The "Spirit-gifted" nature of the Messiah and his reign is fundamental. "And the Spirit of the Lord shall rest upon him" (Is. 11:2). The Spirit was source of discernment, wisdom, and inspiration for all of God's servants in the Old Testament, but particularly God's Anointed (Is. 61:1). The Messiah and also the messianic community of the new era are especially endowed by the Spirit of the Lord (Joel 3:1, 2; cf. Acts 2:16-18). The role of the Holy Spirit in the life and mission of the Messiah is, of course, underscored in the Gospels (Lk. 4:18; 3:16, 22; 4:1, 14).

The essential characteristics with which the coming messianic King is clothed are righteousness and faithfulness (Is. 11:5). Right relationships among each other and with God in the covenant community are God's gifts to his people. The justice, or righteousness, is the concrete form of God's salvation among his people. For that reason the prophets often use the terms "justice" and "salvation" in practically synonymous ways (Is. 59:11; *et al.*).

Faithfulness, or covenant love, more than any other attribute, describes the character and personal identity of God. This trait characterizes both the messianic King and his community. Faithful to his promises, God's Messiah "laid down his life" for humankind, forming a people who by definition are bound in covenant faithfulness to "lay down our lives for the brethren" (1 Jn. 3:16).

The remaining verses (Is. 11:6-9) abound in figures which tell of the life of God's people in the messianic era. Communion among humankind and with God and harmony with nature were lost in the Fall and violence prevailed. The prophets announced that wars and the invasion of foreign powers were, in effect, judgment upon God's people for their infidelities.

On the other hand, the prophetic message of hope looks forward to a change. The messianic era will bring reconciliation between us and God, restore right relationships among persons and harmony with nature. God's messianic salvation includes his kingdom of righteousness in which his peace is established. The instruments of violence will be abolished among God's people who live under his covenant of peace. This strand is picked up in the New Testament. Peter declared that God's message to his people is "the good news of peace by Jesus Christ" (Acts 10:36).

Under the rule of the promised messianic King "they shall not hurt or destroy in all my holy mountain; for the earth shall be full of the knowledge of the Lord as the waters cover the sea" (Is. 11:9). In effect, the Fall and its consequences are reversed in the messianic hope held out by the prophets. The blessings of the messianic era will be universal in their scope and the salvation mediated by this Davidic "branch" shall be for all humanity. This vision which sees the Messiah and his people as the center of God's saving intention for all nations represents an important current in the Bible. In Abraham all of the families of the earth will be blessed (Gen. 12:1-3). "All the nations shall flow . . . to the mountain of the Lord" (Is. 2:2, 3). The Servant of Yahweh is given as "a light to the nations" (Is. 42:4, 6; 49:6). According to the prophets, the ultimate hope for

To be radically right
is to go to the roots.
To foster a society
based on creed
instead of greed,
systematic unselfishness
instead of systematic selfishness,
on gentle personalism
instead of rugged individualism,
is to create a new society
within the shell of the old.

—Peter Maurin

Israel, the coming messianic King, will also be the hope for all nations.

Christians have often been tempted to believe these messianic statements describe a utopia to be fulfilled beyond history as we know it. Although some of these images need to be understood in a figurative sense or, if taken literally, postponed to a period of fulfillment beyond history, others need not be pushed off into the end of time.

Restoration of communion among people and with God has, thanks to Jesus, become a possibility *within human history* in the messianic community. Wherever God's people are willing to live through trust in God, rather than by wealth, status, or violence, they can "beat their swords into plowshares, and their spears into pruning hooks." After all, the true people of God in both covenants owe their life to God's grace rather than to their own capacity to defend themselves.

Undoubtedly the hearers of Isaiah and Micah hoped for the fulfillment *within history* of this vision of God's Anointed and the era of shalom which he would bring. And in the new covenant God's people need not settle for less. In fact, the Holy Spirit enables the Christian community to participate immediately in the messianic blessing which will be realized fully beyond history. The prophetic vision for the future becomes reality when the "shoot from the stump of Jesse and branch out of his roots" appears in the fullness of time as the "true vine."

Conclusion

When judgment finally swept the Southern Kingdom away, Jeremiah and Ezekiel labored to keep true covenant faith alive among God's people. Rooted as they were in Israel's ancient Exodus-Sinai faith, they were able to see beyond the catastrophe. Like Moses, at the close of the Pentateuch, Jeremiah and Ezekiel were granted a glimpse of the future which God had in store for his people—"a new heart . . . and a new spirit." "I will put my law within them, and I will write it upon their hearts; and I will be their God, and they shall be my people"(Ezek. 36:26; Jer. 31:33).

4.
The True Vine Appears

What is the nature of the messianic community as found in the Gospels? We must address this question in order to continue the theme of God's people in the new covenant.

The Gospel writers are unanimous in their conviction about the Messiah. The ruler from David's line, whose coming the prophets had envisioned, had appeared in the person of Jesus of Nazareth. He and his followers are the true vine of God's own planting. His life, death, and resurrection all show signs and examples of how the kingdom of God flourishes upon earth in Jesus himself and in the messianic community which he began. This chapter will explore meanings of becoming God's people in the true vine, Jesus the Messiah.

The Mission of the Messiah

The synoptic writers all include summary statements of Jesus' messianic mission early in their Gospels. In Matthew Jesus announced the gospel of the kingdom with a call to repentance (Mt. 4:17, 23). In Luke repentance meant sharing clothing and food with those in need. For tax collectors it meant becoming more honest and compassionate. For soldiers it meant abandoning their violent and bully tactics for extorting the payment of taxes (Lk. 3:10-14). It was essentially an invitation to return: a radical return to the covenant which God in his love and grace had established with his people.

Biblical repentance is conversion, a radical return to God's will for humankind expressed originally in his good creation, reiterated in his gracious covenant at Sinai, and finally manifested in Jesus. ("Radical," throughout this book, means this return to the original, the root, and does not refer to any contemporary political associations.)

In John we have another description of conditions for entering the kingdom of God which supplements Matthew's. In his conversation with Nicodemus Jesus said it is necessary to be "born anew" to enter the kingdom of God. This new life is not merely a matter of making some outward ethical adjustments. At the same time clearly being "born of the Spirit" issues in deeds being "wrought in God" (Jn. 3:21). From the discussion that follows, it becomes clear that the new birth is the work of God's Spirit and comes through faith (Jn. 3:3-18). Through repentance and faith we are "born anew."

Although life in the kingdom of God was anticipated in the Old Testament jubilee provisions the two covenants had some differences between them. First of all, in the new covenant the Messiah himself has come. God's highest and best word to humankind has been spoken (Heb. 1:1, 2). And furthermore, the powerful role of God's Holy Spirit in his dynamic presence upon Jesus and within the messianic community is a glorious new reality (Lk. 4:14, 18; *et al.;* cf. Jer. 31:33; Ezek. 36:26, 27). Messianic salvation is more than return to jubilee provisions. It moves beyond them because both Jesus and the Spirit have come.

Second, Jesus' call was to peoplehood (Mt. 4:18-22). Although only four are mentioned in this invitation to follow Jesus, the group will eventually number twelve. This group is certainly no mere accident, because these Twelve are representative of the twelve tribes of Israel. Together with the Messiah, these constitute the new people of God.

Ephesians 2 tells of a "new humanity" made up of persons who are very different from one another, even hostile. They are reconciled with one another and with God through the work of Jesus Christ. In the community of the Twelve this new social reality had already come into being. Ex-Zealots and ex-Herodians, who were formerly enemies, now became partners in a movement in which the peace and justice of God are realized. This new humanity, the messianic community created by Jesus, becomes the primary way God works in human history.

Third, Jesus went about "healing every disease and every infirmity among the people" (Mt. 4:23, 24). These healings show that Jesus is the One whom God has authorized to announce and begin the kingdom of heaven (Mt. 9:6; *et al.*). The healings and exorcisms not only set Jesus apart as a miracle worker of extraordinary power, they indicated the *kind* of Messiah he is. When John the Baptist asked, "Are you he who is to come, or shall we look for another," Jesus answered by noting his messianic activity: "The blind receive their sight and the lame walk, lepers are cleansed and the deaf hear, and the dead are raised up, and the poor have good news preached to them" (Mt. 11:4, 5). This clear reply corresponds to Jesus' commissioning to be *this kind* of Messiah at his baptism (Mt. 3:17; Is. 42:1-4). His healing ministry corresponds with the visions in the suffering servant songs of Isaiah. This is the way the New Testament writers interpreted Jesus' amazing healing ministry (Mt. 8:17; 12:15-21; Acts 10:38).

The Mission of the Messianic People, John 15:1-17

Nearly 100 different images of the life and mission of the people of God have been found in the New Testament. One of the most suggestive images in the Gospels for the messianic community is found in John 15:1-17.

This true-vine-and-branches metaphor takes its meaning from the Old Testament. Just as the people of the old covenant depended totally on God for their life and survival, so the people of the new covenant depend absolutely upon Jesus the Messiah for their life and mission. The figure of the vine and

John 15:9-11

"As the Father has loved me, so have I loved you; abide in my love. If you keep my commandments, you will abide in my love, just as I have kept my Father's commandments and abide in his love. These things I have spoken to you, that my joy may be in you, and that your joy may be full."

the branches means that there are no other people of God than the messianic community. "You are" can be decisively said of God's people only in the light of Jesus' messianic "I am."

The relationship of Jesus Christ to the church is similar to the relationship of Yahweh to Israel. In the Old Testament God is the One who reveals himself to his people as the great "I am" (Ex. 3:6, 14; et al.). The Gospel writers applied this formula of self-revelation to Jesus himself. The words with which Jesus appeared to his terrified disciples in Mark 6:50, for example, are translated in the RSV as "it is I." However, the Greek text employs the same formula we find in the Old Testament "I am" passages. Other uses of "I am" in an absolute form with reference to Jesus are found in both Mark and John. However, the use of "I am," together with images referring to Jesus as the Messiah, are especially prominent in John's Gospel: bread of life, living bread, the bread which came down from heaven, light of the world, the door, the Good Shepherd, the resurrection and the life, the way, the truth, and the life.

Therefore, the phrase "I am the true vine" alerts us that as God's Messiah, Jesus' relationship to the church is similar to that of Yahweh to Israel. Jesus is the bearer of salvation, both now and in the future, for the messianic community.

In the Old Testament the vine (or vineyard) had long been used as a symbol of the people of God (Ps. 80:8-18; Is. 5:1-7; 27:2-3; Jer. 2:21; Ezek. 15:2-6; 19:10; Hos. 10:1). In these references the emphasis generally falls on two facts: 1) God's faithfulness in planting and caring for his vineyard and 2) Israel's unfaithfulness which yielded "wild grapes" (Is. 5:1, 2).

In contrast to Israel of old, Jesus declares that he is "the true vine." The primary meaning of the adjective "true" is not a comparison with Israel of old, nor with other contemporary messiah pretenders in first-century Judaism. Here Jesus says, in effect, that he is the true vine in the sense that he alone, as God's Messiah, can be the vine of God's planting. Therefore Jesus is the "true vine" by which all others should be measured and rejected. The ancient Jewish symbol of the vine which had been applied to Israel is now applied to Jesus and to his community.

Jesus is the center of the new community of salvation. The

image of the vine shows graphically how God's salvation, which had formed a people for himself, is all focused in Jesus the Messiah. In the life, death, and resurrection of Jesus, God's saving intention is fully expressed and now the Messiah and his community reach out to embrace all nations, and indeed the universe itself.

In the Old Testament passages which refer to Israel as a vineyard God appears as owner and caretaker (Is. 5:1-3; Jer. 2:21). His relationship to his people of the new covenant has not changed (15:1b). Salvation history throughout both covenants is rooted in God. However, the community of salvation of the new covenant arises out of God's clearest act of self-giving love, Jesus the Messiah.

According to Jewish thought, a grapevine should by its very nature be fruitful (Mt. 3:8, 9; 7:16-20; 12:33). In this story the vinedresser is interested in an abundant harvest. The fruit-bearing described here is not so much the result of the evangelizing mission as the character of their communion with Jesus. The fundamental evangelism mission of the people of God is described in other contexts.) The nature of Israel's fruit-lessness in the Old Testament helps us to understand the fruit-fulness which God expects to find in his new messianic people. In Isaiah 5:1-7 Israel's unfaithfulness to justice and righteousness and the prevalence of violence were concrete forms of fruitlessness. On the other hand, fruitfulness is life according to the values of his kingdom.

This kind of fruit-bearing is fundamental in the life and mission of God's people. Fruitlessness leads to being cut off from the messianic community. God's pruning activity has a purifying effect in keeping with the values of his people. God's intention for his people is that through the work of Christ pruning *(kathairei)* leads to fruitfulness (Jn. 15:2) and the cleansing *(katharoi)*.

Fruitfulness in the messianic community is possible only by God's grace through Christ (Jn. 15:4). Life according to kingdom values, or fruitfulness, is possible through grace. The relationship between Jesus and his disciples is characterized by mutuality. The verb translated "abide" in the RSV occurs ten times in the course of seven verses. It highlights the communion which unites Jesus' disciples to him. Branches

47

Vicit agnus noster, Our lamb has conqu

separated from the stock of the vine are lifeless. It is impossible for them to bear fruit according to covenant values. Only by abiding in his Spirit and his life can Jesus' disciples truly do his works.

Strictly speaking, in this image Jesus is not the stock, or trunk, of the grapevine in contrast to the branches; rather, he is the vine (Jn. 15:5). While we dare not press an allegory too far, in a sense the vine includes the totality of the branches. This unity does not mean that the identities of the Messiah and the members of the messianic community become confused in some sort of mystical union. It means, rather, that Jesus and his disciples are the "Israel of God."

Of course the primacy of Jesus in the messianic community is absolute (Jn. 15:5c). Only by obedient faith in the Messiah does the messianic community of the new covenant take the place of Israel of the old covenant. In the Messiah-with-his-people, God has manifested to the world his fulfillment of the agelong promise made to Abraham.

John 15:9-17 reminds us that God's own love, as he has revealed it in the Messiah, defines the basic nature of his people of the new covenant. Jesus understood the character and form of his love to represent faithfully God's love. And he expected that his followers would reflect in similar ways this same quality of love (Jn. 15:9). In fact, Jesus' "commandments" (i.e., teachings such as we find in Mt. 5 to 7; Lk. 6; et al.) reflect God's love both in its essential nature and in its concrete forms (Jn. 15:10).

Love of the kind which God has shown in Jesus Christ leads to joy in the messianic community (Jn. 15:11). This joy has lit-

eum sequamur.
red, him let us follow.

tle to do with "happiness" as it is generally understood. In the New Testament the relationship of joy to persecution and suffering is especially notable. Christian joy expresses itself as a spontaneous celebration of the new creation. For example, persecution is the world's certification of this new creation.

The concrete love of the messianic community has been clearly demonstrated by Jesus. "This is my commandment, that you love one another as I have loved you. Greater love has no man than this, that a man lay down his life for his friends" (Jn. 15:12, 13). Perhaps the clearest commentary on the meaning of this text is found in 1 John 3:16-18. The form of the pronouns in the Greek text highlights the parallelism John intended between Jesus and his followers. "By this we know love, that *he* laid down his life for us; and *we* ought to lay down our lives for the brethren. But if any one has the world's goods and sees his brother in need, yet closes his heart against him, how does God's love abide in him?"

To love is to "lay down our lives" for others. Rather than being a theoretical definition, Jesus himself filled it with literal content. This love so impressed his disciples that it permeated their lives and writings. In fact, this willingness to suffer on behalf of others is the only aspect of Jesus' life which we are explicitly asked to imitate (1 Pet. 2:20-24; Phil. 2:5-8).

God's people can be defined as that community in which the love of God abounds. This love of God is not merely the church's love for God, or even God's love for his people, although the phrase surely includes these two aspects. The church is that community in which persons, empowered by his Spirit, *love as God loves.* Members are committed to laying

Michael Garde, a member of the Mennonite Community in Dublin, Ireland.

down their very lives for others. Too often in spiritualizing our faith, we have created such a distance between Jesus and his community that we fail to ask the concrete nature of Jesus' love for the church. Yet "laying down his life for his friends" is the form of that love.

Only in the community of the Messiah is death itself stripped of its dreadfulness. God's people are freed from *all* fear. The messianic community is characterized by the joyous abandon whereby we lay down our lives for others. These may be courageous acts of self-sacrifice in extraordinary danger. Or we "lay down our lives" in the day-by-day process of giving our lives in unselfish service to others.

Jesus' death and life are a sign and example of the form of the life and mission of God's people. Jesus' sacrificial death and life of obedience and service are a model for life in the messianic community. "If any man would come after me, let him deny himself and take up his cross and follow me. For whoever would save his life will lose it, and whoever loses his life for my sake will find it" (Mt. 16:24, 25). Jesus' answer to the desire to rule over others by means of force and power is the way of the cross.

The form of this mission also related to Jesus' disciples desire for prestige. "For on the way they had discussed with one another who was the greatest" (Mk. 9:34). Jesus' answer to this grasping desire for prestige is found in the child. "Whoever humbles himself like this child, he is the greatest in the kingdom of heaven" (Mt. 18:4).

But the incident which speaks most eloquently to the problem of desire for power and position is the request of James and John for positions of authority. Jesus' response is clear. "You know that the rulers of the Gentiles lord it over them, and their great men exercise authority over them. It shall not be so among you; but whoever would be great among you must be your servant, and whoever would be first among you must be your slave; even as the Son of man came not to be served but to serve, and to give his life as a ransom for many" (Mt. 20:25-28).

Christians have correctly recognized verse 28 as a statement of Jesus' vicarious death for the salvation of humankind. Because of Jesus' special relationship to God, his death was more than a good example of how his followers should live and die. Jesus redeemed us and reconciled us with God through his death on the cross. He is "the propitiation for our sins." This understanding is found throughout the New Testament, especially in Paul's writings (Gal. 3:10-14; Rom. 3:25; 5:18).

However, the primary intention of the verse in this context is clearly a different one. The term "even as" at the beginning makes it clear that Jesus' life and death function as a model for his followers. In the community of the Messiah we refuse to lord it over others. Rather, we give our lives as servants of God and humanity, *because* Jesus himself lived and died that way. Jesus' life and death is the example for his followers (cf. Jn. 15:12, 13; 1 Jn. 3:16, 17).

Conclusion

The Gospels pick up the vision proclaimed by the prophets of Israel: the Messiah and his people are the instruments of God's salvation for all nations. Jesus' mission is directed to the poor, those dependent on God, the outcasts, and the Gentiles on the fringes of life in first-century Palestine.

The Great Commission, reported in one form or another in each of the Gospels, is by no means temporary or optional, as considerable sectors of the church have imagined at times. Since the day of creation, God's designs have been universal in their scope. Since the call of Abraham, God's purpose for his people has been the blessing of "the nations." The Gospels underscore that Jesus is God's Messiah "for all nations" and that the messianic community is God's people "for all nations" (Mt. 4:15, 16; 28:19; Mk. 11:17; 16:15; Lk. 24:47; *et al.*).

The Messiah with his people is the true vine planted by God. In this vine the agelong promises of God are fulfilled. The universal scope of God's salvation, described in the Gospels, will come to greater fulfillment in the events of Pentecost. This will be the explored of the next chapter.

5.
Branching Out at Pentecost

Pentecost marks the beginning of a new era in the history of salvation. A new community is formed. What is the nature of this community of the people of God? The early chapters of Acts contain three remarkable summary statements of the extraordinary quality of life of the primitive Jerusalem community. These passages (Acts 2:42-47; 4:32-35; 5:12-16) summarize the meaning of Pentecost and serve as a bridge to the rest of Luke's narrative.

Christians generally have assigned relatively little importance to these summaries, seeing them as idealized accounts. It is sometimes claimed that the writer has reported noteworthy incidents in the life of the community in an effort to present near perfect vision of primitive Christianity.

Although biblical records must be interpreted with realism, we should guard against reading the accounts from the viewpoint of the later institutional church. We want to appreciate the wonder and freshness of the Spirit's moving at this new beginning. The New Testament realistically places side by side almost unbelievable descriptions of goodness in the life in the early church, together with embarrassing accounts of human selfishness and sinfulness. As with other passages in the Gospels and epistles we dare not pass these summaries off lightly, simply because they do not fit our values today.

The New Reality: Community

When we compare these summary statements side by side, several characteristics of the Jerusalem church stand out clearly.

1. The primitive Christian community was a fellowship of sharing. This statement may appear redundant because the terms "community," "fellowship," and "sharing" mean practically the same. But this repetition illustrates the broad range of meanings which the term in Acts 2:42 carries. *Koinonia* is translated in the New Testament as fellowship, common, contribution, share, participation, partners, partake, partnership, and generous. It means spiritual as well as material sharing. Its usage in the New Testament makes it clear that koinonia means sharing a common life within the body of Christ at all levels—spiritual, social, intellectual, and economic. No area of life is excluded.

However, repeated references to the material aspects of koinonia in these texts indicate a primary reference to economic sharing. Acts 2:44 shows that it was the practice of the primitive community to share all sorts of things and verse 45 makes it clear that this included in some cases the sale of properties in order to be able to provide for the needy among them. Verse 46 repeats material sharing. In a simple economy the most that common people can aspire to for economic security are shelter, clothing, and a daily ration of food. In such a

Acts 2:42-47

"And they devoted themselves to the apostles' teaching and fellowship, to the breaking of bread and the prayers.

"And fear came upon every soul; and many wonders and signs were done through the apostles. And all who believed were together and had all things in common; and they sold their possessions and goods and distributed them to all, as any had need. And day by day, attending the temple together and breaking bread in their homes, they partook of food with glad and generous hearts, praising God and having favor with all the people. And the Lord added to their number day by day those who were being saved."

society to "[partake] of food [together] with glad and generous hearts" is, in effect, to practice koinonia in a concrete way. In the early church to eat together was communion in a concrete sense.

The second summary underscores the koinonia of the primitive community even more strikingly. Koinonia here includes being of "one heart and soul," renouncing the right to self-centered ownness, sharing all for the common good (Acts 4:32).

Verse 34, apparently a reference to Deuteronomy 15:4, "but there will be no poor among you," emerges from a jubilee context (Deut. 15:1-11). Under the Holy Spirit the Jerusalem community was continuing the jubilee practices which Jesus had announced and had begun to carry out in the circle of his disciples (Lk. 4:18).

Clearly the text shows that sharing was voluntary; a general economic leveling was not imposed. Many freely abandoned legitimate claims to possessions out of love for their brothers and sisters. The form of the verbs in the Greek text indicates that the property sales to meet needs in the community were a repeated action over an extended period of time. Thus we understand that often "they sold their possesions" (Acts 2:45) and were in the habit of regularly bringing "the proceeds of what was sold" (Acts 4:34). Western Christians have rarely asked with any seriousness what texts such as these might mean for the church. At face value they would appear to mean, at the very least, unlimited and unconditional economic liability and total financial availability to brothers and sisters in the Christian community.

2. All three summaries underscore that the primitive Christian congregation was a community of healing (Acts 2:43; 4;33; 5:12, 15, 16). The healing activity is described and interpreted more fully in chapters 3 and 4. The lame man at the temple gate was healed "in the name of Jesus Christ of Nazareth" (Acts 3:6) and Peter, in interpreting the event, did not hesitate to ascribe this "wonder" to Jesus, the suffering servant Messiah. (Other references to this motif are Acts 3:1, 13; referring to Isaiah 52:13; 53:12 and Acts 3:26; 4:27-30, referring to Psalm 2:1,2.)

This healing activity is described repeatedly as "signs and

wonders" and "power." Jesus' healings were interpreted in the Gospels as evidence that he was the Messiah according to the suffering servant vision of Isaiah, as well as a sure sign that the kingdom of God had come. The meaning of "signs and wonders" in the primitive community is unmistakable. Jesus' messianic community continues his ministry of healing. These healings and exorcisms continue to be signs of the presence of the kingdom and of its victorious struggle against evil (Acts 4:27-31). According to Acts, the healing ministry of the community of the servant Messiah continues the mission of its servant Lord.

3. The first summary emphasizes that the early Christian congregation was a worshiping community (Acts 2:42, 46, 47). The common life of the brotherhood was encouraged by an ongoing program of apostolic teaching to interpret the values and meaning of the messianic age (Acts 2:42). Apostolic teaching was fundamental to the new church because it provided an authentic link between Jesus and the Pentecostal community of the Spirit.

Prayer was an essential ingredient in the life of the early Christian community. Judging from the early chapters of Acts, prayer was both personal and communal, formal and spontaneous. The phrase in 2:42, "the prayers," seems to indicate that they were not merely general prayers. Furthermore, regular temple attendance in this early period would scarcely have been totally independent of the temple's worship forms (2:46). In fact, it is specifically reported that the healing of the lame man occurred while Peter and John were on their way "to the temple at the hour of prayer" (Acts 3:1; cf. 5:12).

On the other hand, their free and grateful praise surely must have differed from the traditional cultic forms (2:47). The community's prayer reported in Acts 4:24-31 reflects the realism of a people who know that they have been called to be God's community in the midst of a world at war with the Messiah. In this context the prayers of God's people are really earthshaking events with cosmic as well as historic consequences (Acts 4:31).

Although the messianic community in Jerusalem continued to participate in at least some aspects of temple worship after Pentecost, one receives the impression that the Pentecostal community's worship moved beyond Jewish cultic forms. The temple was no longer the real center of worship practice. The new center of the Spirit was in the houses where brothers and sisters met to break bread together, to pray, to share food with glad and generous hearts, and to praise God (Acts 2:46, 47a).

4. The summaries also report that the primitive church was a witnessing community. All aspects of the life of the community carried witness value. The outstanding aspects of koinonia and worship were apparently effective, for the "Lord added to their number day by day those who were being saved" (Acts 2:47b). Worship in the face of adversity contributed to the "boldness" with which they gave their witness (Acts 4:31). And the healing ministry of the messianic community resulted in testimony (Acts 4:33) and in numerical growth (Acts 5:14).

These summary statements also help interpret the narratives of the early chapters of acts the way the writer Luke intended. Acts 2:43-47 provides clues to interpret the story of Pentecost in chapter 2. The second summary (Acts 4:32-35) provides additional perspective on chapter 2, as well as on the experience of Barnabas and Ananias and Sapphira (Acts 4:36-5:11). The third summary (Acts 5:12-16), and to some extent the first and second (Acts 2:43; 4:33), shed light on the meaning of the healing of the lame man and the confrontation with the powers that followed (Acts 3:1—4:31).

A widespread tendency among Christians is to view Pentecost only from a standpoint of asking whether such incidents continue to happen to persons in the modern era. (A similar attitude toward healings and exorcisms in the New Testament is revealed when we ask whether they really happened and can be expected to occur today.) Our observations on the summary statements in Acts may anticipate the biblical response. These statements are really biblical *interpretations* of events.

Therefore, what really happened at Pentecost was the outpouring of the Holy Spirit. This led to the formation of a new covenant community of the Spirit. Because God had poured out his Spirit upon these men and women, he made possible koinonia in its fullest dimensions. They had a vertical relationship of communion with God and a horizontal relationship of communion with brothers and sisters.

Church of the Brethren youth at Estes Park, Colorado, in 1979.

Sometimes, given our North American setting and our belief in the freedom of the will, we give the greatest share of our attention to the human part of Pentecost. But believers can be a fellowship of sharing and caring only because they have individually and as a group shared in God's grace. By God's grace the community of the Holy Spirit became a reality at Pentecost. This meant liberation from the powers of evil in all of their forms.

The Community of the Spirit

The issue of tongues occupies a prominent place in the Pentecost narrative (Acts 2:3-11). Whatever the exact nature of these tongues may have been, the passages seem to underscore that without them communication would have been impossible. Luke apparently intended that speaking and hearing in different tongues should be understood to refer to the confusion of languages at Babel. This parallel would have been particularly noticeable to Jews familiar with the Greek version of the Old Testament. The Greek word translated "bewildered" in the RSV (Acts 2:6) is from the same root as the verb translated "confuse" in Genesis 11:7, 9. Whereas at Babel rebellion ended in confusion, at Pentecost God's Spirit transformed confusion into understanding. Luke wanted his readers to understand that the Spirit's presence has reversed Babel. Just as God's answer to humanity's rebellious confusion had been a new kind of people—Abraham and his children—so in the messianic era God's answer to human sinfulness is the new community of the Spirit.

Furthermore, the text shows a parallel to the Exodus-Sinai story which clarified Israel's peoplehood. The Pentecost narrative is sprinkled with references to "the mighty works of God" (Acts 2:11, 22) "and wonders and signs" (Acts 2:19, 22, 43). For Greek-speaking Jews of the first century these terms were familiar. In the Old Testament these phrases almost always referred to Moses leading the people out of Egypt and to the special circumstances under which God Almighty showed Israel to be his chosen people. These phrases formed part of Israel's ancient creed (Deut. 26:5-9). As part of Israel's worship, they were continually present in the memory of God's people.

For Luke, the new age of redemption is confirmed in the

reappearance of "signs and wonders." Just as the Exodus redemption and forming of God's covenant people at Sinai were characterized by "signs and wonders," the "signs and wonders" of the new era also refer to messianic salvation and the formation of a new community of the Spirit.

Although the Pentecostal manifestations of the Spirit in fire, wind, and speaking in other tongues have a rich and varied symbolic use in the Old Testament and other Jewish writings, the primary symbolism which Luke intended is undoubtedly the Exodus experience. In the Exodus, God was manifested in a "pillar of fire" (Ex. 13:21, 22; 14:24). Now again a special presence manifests itself resting upon each one of them in the new Israel (Acts 2:3). "A strong east wind" dried up the sea making it passable (Ex. 14:21) and now the house in which the disciples met was filled with "a sound ... like the rush of a mighty wind" (Acts 2:2). Because in both Hebrew and Greek the words for wind and Spirit are identical, this identification was natural for original readers.

Judaism also had a tradition which celebrated the giving of the law at Pentecost. Thus the marvelous manifestation of divine power at Pentecost would have reminded Jewish readers of Sinai and pointed to the new reality which God was creating in fulfillment of his promise, "I will put my spirit within you, and cause you to walk in my statutes and be careful to observe my ordinances" (Ezek. 36:27; cf. Jer. 31:31-34). Just as Israel of old had received a new identity as the people of God at Sinai through the gift of the law, so now, a new people of God is formed by the gift of his Spirit.

This Exodus symbolism clearly must have been in the mind of Luke and obvious to his readers. The implications are important for us, since Pentecost is of crucial importance to the church's understanding of itself. At Pentecost the fundamental work of the Spirit of God was the formation of the new community of the messianic era. In this community persons find wholeness and salvation.

In his Pentecost sermon Peter gives considerable attention to Jesus' life, death, and resurrection as the basis for the forgiveness of sins. In fact, this is a common feature in the sermons recorded in the Books of Acts. The unanimous testimony of the apostolic witnesses declares that the death of Jesus is for our salvation (Rom. 4:25; Heb. 2:9; 9:26b; *et al.*). The New Testament writers used a variety of metaphors to describe this atonement which makes possible communion both with God and others within the community of the Spirit.

The Spirit grants individuals a new dignity precisely because of their participation in his community. According to Acts 2:2 the tongues of fire were "distributed and resting on each one of them." What in the old covenant had been the lot of kings and prophets, and finally, of the Messiah himself, has now become the privilege of the entire messianic community.

The Spirit's coming makes it possible for us to overcome all the old distinctions which separated persons: class, sex, and age (Acts 2:17, 18). The Apostle Paul would report this new equality, noting that through Christ all are descendants of promise so that there is neither Jew nor Greek, slave nor free, male nor female (Gal. 3:28). It is the era of the new covenant written on every heart (Jer. 31:31-34). However, the Pentecost narrative shows us that all this is possible only in the new community of the Spirit which God is creating.

The New Creation

A striking image which helps us understand salvation within the new community of the Spirit is the metaphor of the "new creation." Paul wrote, "With us therefore worldly standards have ceased to count in our estimate of any man. . . . And for anyone who is in Christ, there is a new creation; the old creation has gone, and now the new one is here" (2 Cor. 5:16, 17, *Jerusalem Bible,* cf. NEB).

The Greek term translated "creation" in this text is the one most commonly used in the New Testament. In its verb form it is used exclusively to refer to creation as an act of God. The term translated "new" means new in kind, or distinctive, as opposed to newness in time. The new creation is the glorious culmination of God's creative and saving purpose. As in Galatians 6:15 "new creation" here has to do with a totally new order, not only the created order of things and persons, but also the orientation from which we view reality and measure values. This new creation, as well as the old, is affected by the Word and the Spirit (Gen. 1:1-3; Eph. 2:15).

The new creation image helps us to understand the inten-

Gemeinschaft is a German ter[m] equivalent. It denotes the in[?] a group shares some deep com[m] experience has been that bandin[g] following him on his way to th[e] ality possible and so the sourc[e] we can know; that the Brethre[n] is not entirely coincidental.

tion and the dimensions of Peter's warning, "Save yourselves from this crooked generation" (Acts 2:40). The term translated "generation" may mean a race, or a people, bound together by a common heritage. However, in the New Testament it generally refers to contemporary society in a negative sense. A collective term, it is aimed at a whole group of people rather than merely at individuals.

Negatively stated, Peter calls on his hearers to repent, that is, to change radically and be saved from their contemporary society. It is misdirected and has false values. The saving alternative was the new community (Acts 2:42) which had come into being through God's Word and Spirit. The orientation and values of the community of the new creation are outlined in the summaries which we have already examined (Acts 2:42-47; *et al.*).

Another aspect of the new creation is underscored in Galatians 6:15, 16: "For neither circumcision counts for anything, nor uncircumcision, but a new creation. Peace and mercy be upon all who walk by this rule, upon the Israel of God." The parallel passage in Ephesians 2:14, 15 sheds additional light

r which there is no adequate English
ate sense of union that comes as
ment in common. The Brethren
gether as the people of the Lord,
ingdom is the profoundest common-
f the greatest Gemeinschaft
aue been known as "the Brethren"

-- Vernard Eller

on the meaning of this new creation: "For he is himself our peace. Gentiles and Jews, he has made the two one, and in his own body of flesh and blood has broken down the enmity which stood like a dividing wall between them; for he annulled the law with its rules and regulations, so as to create out of the two a single new humanity in himself, thereby making peace" (NEB). This new creation, or new humanity, is a new social reality. In it the most formidable of all the barriers of the ancient world, the one separating Jews and Gentiles, has been overcome.

The New Testament reflects the conviction that there are only two "humanities": the new humanity and the old (Eph. 4:22; Col. 3:9). And the only acceptable alternative to the old humanity is the radically new option of the new creation, the new community of the Spirit.

Conclusion

In Acts 2 the development of the new community of the Spirit formed of "men from every nation under heaven" (2:5) goes in two directions. On one hand, it picks up the Old Testa-

63

ment vision of the people of God who are a blessing and a light to all nations (Gen. 12:3; Is. 42:4, 6). On the other hand, it looks forward to the vision with which the New Testament closes.

And they sang a new song saying,
"Worthy art thou to take the scroll and to open its seals,
For thou wast slain and by thy blood didst ransom men for God
From every tribe and tongue and people and nation. . . .

"Behold, the dwelling of God is with men.
He will dwell with them,
And they shall be his people,
And God himself will be with them" (Rev. 5:9; 21:3)

The vision of the community of the Spirit described on the pages of the New Testament has continued on throughout Christian history. It has often been dimmed by the church's temptation to adapt itself to fallen social values. But it has survived particularly in those Christian movements which have been renewed by the Spirit and the Word. Such renewal movements will be the subject of the next two chapters.

6.
Branching Out
in Renewal Movements

Four titles which described Israel of old were "a chosen race, a royal priesthood, a holy nation, [and] God's own people." These titles now refer to the new community of the Messiah (1 Pet. 2:9, 10). At the very center of this apostolic vision of God's people is his ongoing purpose for the church ("that you may declare the wonderful deeds of him who called you out of darkness into his marvelous light"). Unfortunately, the nature and calling of God's people have not always shone forth with such clarity in the history of the church. Because of the church's contacts with Greek culture and philosophy, pagan thoughts and values began to color the church's understanding of itself.

The Christian church resisted the pressures and persecution of the Roman Empire for nearly three centuries. But when toleration was finally granted, followed by a gradual increase in status and privilege, the church could not resist the pressure to conform. Christians gradually compromised and accepted society's values as their own. Rather than allowing its life and mission to be radically shaped by the gospel and the values of the kingdom which Jesus had begun, the church gradually adapted to the values of the society around it. In an attempt to insure its own survival and relevance in the world, the church, ironically, came close to losing both. Approximately three centuries after its beginning in the New

Testament, the persecuted church became a persecuting church.

This remarkable change in the life of the church has been called Constantinianism, for the Roman emperor who initiated the policy of toleration and privilege toward the Christians. Constantinianism has become so common for Western Christianity that its far-reaching effects are taken for granted by most Christians in the world.

However, sensitive Christian minorities throughout the church's history have considered the Constantinian alliance to be the fall of the church. Time and again the conscience of the church has been stirred by groups of Christians who were moved by the Spirit of God. The groups noted in this chapter are not considered to be an exhaustive list but do provide representative examples. They have caught a fresh glimpse of God's intention for his people revealed with crystal clarity in Jesus through the Gospels and the messianic community of the New Testament. These groups have called the church to authentic repentance: to return to its roots found in Christ's coming and in the messianic community of the first century.

To provide this alternate history of the church is not to say that God's Spirit has not also worked through mainstream church history. Believers' churches owe much to the heritage of the larger Jewish and Christian community. But the intent here is to celebrate the gift which radical Christianity can bring to the world. Only by returning to their roots have Christians gained the perspective which has enabled them to recognize and unmask the many forms of fallenness in the church.

1 Peter 2:9, 10

"But you are a chosen race, a royal priesthood, a holy nation, God's own people, that you may declare the wonderful deeds of him who called you out of darkness into his marvelous light. Once you were no people but now you are God's people; once you had not received mercy but now you have received mercy."

Montanists

Shortly after the year 150 the Montanist movement appeared in Asia Minor with a renewed emphasis on the role of the Holy Spirit in the ongoing life of the church. They emphasized holiness of life and held a lively hope in the second coming. The renewal movement of these "men of the Spirit," as Tertullian called them, arose as a reaction to the tendency of the church to adapt itself to a Greco-Roman culture and values.

In order to validate its existence the church increasingly looked to the past, assured by the apostolic succession of canon, creed, and fixed leadership. The Montanists also looked to the future, enlightened by the lively hope of the Lord's coming and to the present, nurtured by the charismatic gifts of the Spirit.

The Montanist movement was basically a protest against this "institutionalization" of authority in the church. With Scriptures in hand these believers expected to hear the voice of the living Spirit of God in their midst. Christians of the stature of Tertullian and Irenaeus warned the church not to "quench this movement of the Spirit." Although it disappeared several centuries later, its spirit lived on in other movements.

Donatists

Around AD 315 a movement arose in the church in North Africa calling the brotherhood to a more evangelical discipline. The period of persecution had passed and it was considerably easier to be a Christian. The Donatists, as this movement was called, feared for the consequences of this moral and ethical laxness in the life of the church. They also questioned the growing sacramental forms which accompanied this relaxation of morals. When Constantine attempted to intervene in the life of the church in North Africa they raised the obvious question, "What does the emperor have to do with the church?" About one century later the Donatists were forcibly "recatholicized" by imperial agents in the service of the established church. The church father, Augustine, had spent considerable energy combating these early advocates of the "believers' church." He urged the agents on with the text "compel people to come in" (Lk. 14:23).

Monasticism

From the third century onward monasticism was another way in which sensitive Christians could concretely express their concern about the life of the church. Monasticism arose in part from a concern that the church was giving in to secularism and the surrounding culture. The monastic protest took several forms. Sometimes individuals simply withdrew from society. Sometimes they formed communities in which they attempted to practice the disciplines of evangelical (gospel) life.

In contrast to an increasingly secularized Christianity, the monks took the teachings of Jesus, including the Sermon on the Mount, seriously. In spite of certain excesses and abuses, monasticism at its best represents an attempt to renew the church by offering a more evangelical alternative. The principal weakness of monasticism lies in its failure to more seriously challenge the institutional church to change.

Waldensians

Toward the close of the twelfth century the Waldensian movement arose in Southern France in response to the itinerant preaching of Peter Waldo. A profound conversion led him to share his wealth and dedicate himself to itinerant preaching and a life of radical discipleship. The contribution of Peter Waldo consisted in his application of the "evangelical counsels" of poverty and obedience (discipleship) to all Christians, and not merely to the monks. Patterning their lifestyle after the New Testament, the Waldensians tried to interpret it simply and directly. The Gospels and the Sermon on the Mount in particular furnished models for their discipleship. This brought them into conflict with many of the practices of the medieval church, especially in regards to coercive power and the accumulation of wealth. They did not glorify economic austerity as a value in and of itself, but rather practiced simple living in the interest of their missionary calling.

Reading the New Testament led them to reject violence, including capital punishment. Their commitment to God and his kingdom led them to refuse to swear the loyalty oaths which civil authorities required of their subjects. Their witness was so effective that the movement spread throughout South and Central Europe, in spite of extremely fierce persecution.

Lollards

During the last part of the fourteenth century a renewal movement arose in England which spread by a community of unlicensed itinerant preachers characterized by their evangelical poverty. The Lollards were notable for their insistence on biblical authority for their faith and practice. Although there are no known links between the earlier Waldensians of Southern Europe and the Lollards, they shared remarkable similarities. The Lollards arrived at notably radical conclusions through their intentionally unsophisticated and immediate recourse to the Scriptures.

The principal spokesman for this movement was John Wycliffe, England's foremost theologian of the period. Wycliffe was largely responsible for providing the movement with an English version of the Scriptures, as well as the tracts which the traveling preachers used in proclaiming the gospel.

The movement became so popular among the common people that at one point one of its opponents exclaimed, probably with exaggerated alarm, that half the people of England were Lollards! Opposition forced the movement underground within a generation, but it persisted until the beginnings of the Reformation more than a century later. In fact, several centuries later Baptists, Independents, and Quakers flourished in precisely those areas where the Lollard movement had been the strongest.

The biblical radicalism of Wycliffe was notable as he sharply critiqued the institutional church. He held that secular power and temporal wealth were the twin sources of the "poison which filled the church." Wycliffe preached the biblical principle of wealth which holds that God is Owner of all, and that, as humans, we are no more than stewards charged with the care and responsible use of the earth's resources. Wycliffe also provided a biblical critique of the violence and hunger for power which he noted among Christians. Only eleven years after his death, his followers presented the first pacifist petition to come before the House of Commons, based essentially on the Sermon on the Mount. Following his death in 1384, Wycliffe's bones as well as his books were burned by a church which could not tolerate such biblical teaching.

Christ Jesus says, "Count well the cost
When you lay the foundation."
Are you resolved, though all seem lost,
To risk your reputation,
Your self, your wealth, for Christ the Lord
As you now give your solemn word?

Into Christ's death you're buried now
Through baptism's joyous union.
No claim of self dare you allow
If you desire communion
With Christ's true church, His willing bride,
Which through His Word, He has supplied.

       – Alexander Mack

Czech Brethren

During the fifteenth century, Bohemia was caught in a violent religious and social struggle for the soul of the nation. Finally, out of the ruins of a fierce war a renewal movement called the Unity of the Czech Brethren formed around the spiritual leadership of Peter Chelcicky. The movement represented a radical return to the New Testament for which the interpretive key was the person of Jesus understood through his life and teachings.

The "law of love" which Jesus summarized and the Sermon on the Mount were especially important. Although the state resorts to violence, the church uses love as its instrument of persuasion. It was Chelcicky's conviction that Constantinianism which placed the exercise of power at the service of the church had led to its downfall. For that reason he advocated a clear separation between the church and the state.

Chelcicky's critique of medieval society was equally daring. He insisted that the social and economic inequalities perpetrated in medieval society and defended by the established church were the opposite of the biblical vision for God's people. The movement was especially characterized by its common social and economic life based on its reading of the New Testament.

The Spanish Alumbrados

The "illuminated ones," so-called by their enemies, was a movement of practical lay Christianity which arose in Spain around the year 1500. The evangelical piety of the movement was based on its recovery of the Scriptures, and above all, the Gospels and the epistles. The movement was characterized by small groups of women and men who gathered around the Scriptures for instruction in discipleship, worship, and mutual edification. The Sermon on the Mount was viewed as essential for instruction in the Christian way. They were led to a radical biblical stance in relation to a number of the issues of their time: swearing loyalty oaths, use of force in evangelism, and enforcement of orthodoxy, clericalism, sacramentalism, and a "works salvation".

The movement—called Catholic Evangelism by later his-

Jan Luycken

Renewal leaders (clockwise from top left): **John Wycliffe,** reformer and Bible translator who inspired the Lollard movement in 14th-century England. **Peter Waldo,** pre-Reformation leader who inspired the Waldensian movement. **Conrad Grebel,** a leader of the Swiss Brethren movement which emerged in Switzerland in the 1520s. **Geoge Fox,** early leader of the Quaker movement in

17th-century England. **Menno Simons,** a former village priest in Friesland who joined the Anabaptist movement in 1536. **Annekan Hendriks,** an Anabaptist martyr who was burned in Amsterdam in 1571. **Alexander Mack,** a founder of the Church of the Brethren in Swartznau, Germany, in 1708.

torians—was crushed in Spain by the Inquisition which destroyed the communities which had formed in two of the principal cities. Leaders and participants alike were condemned to imprisonment and death at the stake. Only those who had fled from Spain earlier escaped with their lives. The movement lived on for a time in Italy attracting a number of notable persons of the period. The principal exponent of the movement was the Spaniard, Juan de Valdés. He and the movement presented a doctrine and practice of salvation by faith alone, which by its very nature flowers in the values of authentic righteousness. As with other truly radical movements in sixteenth-century Europe, the Spanish Alumbrados were persecuted mercilessly by Catholics and Protestants alike.

Anabaptism

During the Protestant Reformation in Europe in the early 1520s, a renewal movement, later called Anabaptism, emerged. It shared many of the emphases of these earlier movements. Because the groups publishing this study—the Church of the Brethren, the Brethren in Christ, and the Mennonites—all trace their spiritual roots to this movement, it is appropriate to give more attention to its contributions. It will be the subject of the next chapter.

Society of Friends

A radical renewal movement which appeared in mid-seventeenth-century England called itself the Society of Friends. By their detractors they were called Quakers. By all counts Quakerism was a remarkable religious movement of the period. Responding to the spiritual needs of seventeenth-century England, Quakerism became the fastest-growing religious movement in the West during the first forty years of its existence.

The secret of Quakerism's attraction is found in its New Testament simplicity. To be a Christian was to have passed from death to life. This Christian fellowship had no laypeople in the generally accepted sense of the term. All Christians are ministers, servants of one another. And the church is the living community of God's people.

Perhaps the most remarkable contribution of Quakerism is

74

found in its understanding of its life and mission as participation in "the war of the Lamb." This metaphor describes their participation with Christ against all the forms of evil, within the heart of persons as well as in the evil structures of human society. They used the weapons of the Lamb—love and long-suffering patience. Based on the gospel and their own experience they believed that truth and love will prevail over error and evil. With this joyful certainty, they became missionaries carrying their appeal literally to the ends of the earth.

An Example Today

Contemporary examples of the church being faithful to its calling can also be cited. We are all acquainted with movements which reflect remarkably the Spirit, word, and deeds of Jesus, as well as the characteristics of the New Testament messianic community. These include certain indigenous Christian movements found throughout the world, inner-city communities of mission, certain renewed congregations, and a wide variety of radical Christian communities. The "comunidades cristianas" of Burgos (Spain) are, in many ways, representative of these movements of renewal in our time.

The Christian communities of Burgos are a network of cell groups made up of about 300 persons who live in one of Spain's most traditionally clerical and militaristic cities. Beginning as a youth movement, they have come to include a number of young families and a sprinkling of other adults. Undoubtedly, they are still more of a movement than a church. They are organized into "communities of faith" for purposes of Bible study, worship and witness, and mutual encouragement in their discipleship. The centers of the movement are several "communities of living" in which their common life under the lordship of Christ is shared more intensely. They practice economic sharing, common decision-making, mutual responsibility and common mission. Their radical commitment and lack of organization make them suspect to both Catholics and Protestants.

A closer look at the community reveals a number of characteristics which give a New Testament tone to their life and mission. They are committed to daily disciple obedience,

Kermit Thomasson

S. F. Pannabecker

(Clockwise from top left): **C. N. Hostetter,** chairman of Mennonite Central Committee (1955-68) and former president of Messiah College. **Dan West,** Church of the Brethren, founder of Heifer Project and peace spokesman. **J. J. Thiessen,** president of Canadian Mennonite Conference for 25 years and a founder of Canadian Mennonite Bible College. **P. C. Hiebert,** chairman of Mennonite Central Committee for 33 years. **B. B. Janz** (1877-1964), Men-

nonite Brethren leader in Russia and North America; **Rowena and James Lark,** Mennonite church planters in Illinois and California. **Harold S. Bender,** dean of Goshen College and Mennonite historian who stated the Anabaptist vision. **Martha R. Burkhalter,** General Conference Mennonite Church missionary in India for 30 years. **Sarah Hoover Bert,** cofounder of the Brethren in Christ mission in Chicago, 1894.

even praying for grace to reject the temptation to try to assure their own institutional survival. In following their calling their stance is one of apostolic poverty. Humanly speaking, they are among the poorest and the weakest in their neighborhoods. But this missionary vulnerability leaves those they serve and to whom they witness fully free and not forced to receive the gospel.

These seemingly weak communities of discipleship and healing are, in reality, the community of the Spirit, depending ultimately on God for their life and mission.

Conclusion

Although we have described these movements in positive terms, we must guard against idealizing them uncritically. Even the best movements are subject to the problems of fallen humanity. The Donatists and Wycliffe played into the hands of the nationalism of their times. Many have had difficulty maintaining an adequate balance between the authority of the Spirit and the letter of the written Word. Most have had tensions in finding an adequate balance between spontaneity and structure. All church renewal movements have a built-in tendency to shape their forms only in reaction to the problems which they are trying to reform.

Nonetheless, these representative movements offer real alternatives to a broad spectrum of problems and issues. They show occasions of the people of God branching out again and again from an apparently lifeless religious structure.

The value of these and other similar movements does not lie in their ability to survive and project themselves institutionally. Some of these movements have not survived. And those which have are among the smallest of the denominational groups within Christendom. Their gift or value lies, rather, in their radicality, in the quality of their prophetic message.

The history of the Christian church tells us that no church form is free from moral and doctrinal ambiguities. The people of God in all ages are called to repentance and to faithful obedience. They do this based on their roots in Jesus and the messianic community of the New Testament and in view of God's mission in the world. The people of God are those who live by his mercy (1 Pet. 2:10).

7.
Branching Out Through Anabaptism

The Evangelical Anabaptists of the sixteenth century are one of the clearest examples of radical renewal from church history. This does not mean that the Anabaptists saw more clearly the nature of the gospel, nor that they were more obedient disciples than Christians of other centuries. Rather, due to the broad range of church options present in sixteenth-century Europe, they were a clear example of a radical Christian alternative.

Evangelical Anabaptism arose out of the context of the Protestant Reformation. It shared the fundamental tenets of the Reformation: the authority of Scripture and salvation by faith. Early Anabaptists freely recognized their indebtedness to Zwingli and Luther, as well as Erasmus. However, their main difference with the Reformers was their conviction that these did not take their reform far enough.

They wanted to carry out the principles which Luther and Zwingli had called for early in their lives as Reformers. Luther wrote of the possibility of an "evangelical order" which would have freed the church from the ancient Constantinian alliance and opened the way for the restoration of a covenant community of disciples. Zwingli had spoken of making decisions in the local congregation. However, when this ideal was sacrificed in favor of giving authority in spiritual matters to the prince and the municipal council, the Anabaptists protested in the interests of a New Testament vision of the church.

With the passage of time and as Anabaptism spread, various groups emerged. These included the Hutterites, Mennonites, Amish, Brethren, Brethren in Christ, and today what are sometimes called "radical evangelicals." These groups look to Anabaptism for inspiration of an example of a movement which in many ways embodied the basic elements of New Testament Christianity. Three of these renewal movements will be noted in this survey of Anabaptism.

In seventeenth-century Germany a movement called Pietism brought renewed spirituality and obedience to many Christians. Personal spiritual experience, a deeper interest in Bible study and prayer, a new seriousness in the ethical dimensions of the Christian life, and a missionary conviction stood out in contrast to the usual practices of contemporary churches.

The movement which came to be called the Church of the Brethren arose principally in southwestern Germany at the beginning of the eighteenth century. Early leaders of the movement were influenced by the church historian, Gottfried Arnold, who had written descriptions of the life and belief of the primitive church. He held that later Christians should follow these same teachings. Influenced by the Anabaptists—and their enemies mistook them to be Anabaptists—the group was led to covenant church membership through believers' baptism. They established the agape feast, as well as other ordinances which were viewed as signs of brotherhood. Reading the New Testament led them to thoroughgoing nonresistance, fraternal economic practices, and discipleship.

In the late eighteenth century in eastern Pennsylvania a Christian movement emerged in which leaders called for a heart-felt Christian experience and obedience to the New Testament. This emphasis on Pietism and obedience led what came to be called the Brethren in Christ Church to regain some of the missionary earnestness which had been a part of earlier Anabaptism.

A nineteenth-century writer said they "met together in council, and after deep meditation and discarding all human creeds, took the unadulterated Word of the Lord as a guide, seeking to follow the primitive teachings of Christ and the apostles." The Brethren in Christ sought to bring together a New Testament emphasis on a joyful piety, thoroughgoing discipleship, and holy living.

Among the Mennonite colonies in mid-nineteenth-century Russia the church had taken on some Constantinian forms. A movement arose which was to bring renewal to New Testament teachings and to the original elements of Anabaptism. Initially inspired by a German Lutheran Pietist Eduard Wüst, who emphasized God's grace and holy living, the movement spread to a concern for greater expression of faith in an open and free manner and a concern for moral and ethical laxness among church members.

This renewal, which sometimes developed excesses in emotionalism and individualism, nevertheless was an attempt to give a greater New Testament character to the church. The movement brought renewal to the Mennonite colonies and the Mennonite Brethren Church. It emphasized Bible study, personal conversion, discipleship, a corrective discipline, and missionary outreach.

Today the various Mennonite groups, the Brethren in Christ, and the Church of the Brethren continue to branch out as spiritual descendants of Anabaptism. In the meantime, many younger Christian groups have discovered the Anabaptist story and tradition, often living its essence with greater vitality than some of the older churches. The point of this chapter is not to comment directly on these various Christian communities today. The intent is rather to lift up the contributions this example of authentic Christian renewal can make to others as well as to ourselves.

Voluntary Membership

The Anabaptists insisted on a free church, free in a double sense: 1) made up of voluntary membership and 2) independent from official social structures in organization, authority, and membership. This aspect of the Anabaptist vision greatly troubled the Reformers, as well as the Catholics. They feared that society would become pagan and the church would collapse if they did not have an alliance with political power. Therefore the question of believers' baptism became the central issue in the conflict, and the dissidents were called

"Anabaptists" instead of "brethren," as they called themselves. Of course, this kind of church is not ultimately concerned about becoming a large and powerful body. Such concerns are reserved for the church which is allied with power in society and whose baptism is, in a sense, involuntary.

The essential meaning of believer's baptism is not only that all believers must have a faith of their own. It also describes the nature of the church. Its membership must be free and voluntary, and its sole loyalty is to Christ. As Menno Simons suggested, only in a church whose membership is voluntary can brotherly love be an essential part. By its very nature, brotherly love cannot be forced upon a congregation. Therefore all forms of coercion and force in forming the church were rejected by the Anabaptists from the very beginning of the movement.

Binding and Loosing

Discipleship is nurtured in the believers' church through exercising fraternal discipline. Luther himself had noted that fraternal discipline in the context of a Christian congregation is possible only in a church whose members "seriously want to be Christian." Fraternal discipline, the believers' church alternative to official discipline, was considered essential by early Anabaptists. In his *Rules for Congregational Order* Michael Sattler wrote that it is the duty and obligation of each and every believer to admonish in a Christian and fraternal way an erring brother or sister.

Conrad Grebel insisted on the practice of believers' baptism because: "We understand that not even an adult should be baptized without the rule of Christ of binding and loosing." In this particular reference to believer's baptism and emphasis does not fall on what kind of emotional experience is associated with genuine conversion, or at what age a person has the capacity to experience conversion. Rather, baptism is for those who have been "born anew," and through Christ have a new kind of life, attitude, will, and commitment to submit to each other and accept responsibility for the spiritual well-being of their brothers and sisters. A believer should be baptized when he or she is able (and willing) to practice the rule of

Christ (Mt. 18:15-20).

Balthasar Hubmaier wrote that where fraternal discipline is missing, no true believers' Church exists, even though there may be baptism and the Lord's Supper. Loving concern for the well-being of others is the believers' church alternative to the exercise of discipline which is punishing, repressive, or "to teach a lesson." Kingdom discipline played an essential role in the Anabaptist understanding of the church because they did not claim perfection. It was a fully human community of brothers and sisters whose love for one another took concrete reconciling and healing form.

Community Ethic

The Anabaptists' extraordinary quality of life was seen by their neighbors. In fact, if persons were especially serious in their moral and social behavior, this was reason enough to suspect them of being Anabaptists. But what was even more radical in the Anabaptist concept of holiness of life was the group context in which it was expressed. Besides being transformed individuals, a new social reality had been created. Salvation was experienced in a covenanted community in which life was lived according to the model which Jesus had lived and taught. Christendom generally considered this impossible.

Resources for holy living were released in the covenant community. This emphasized the differences between the two kingdoms. In the perfection of Christ, as living in Christ's kingdom was sometimes called, relationships were characterized by self-giving love. Outside the perfection of Christ, social relationships were assured by use of force, violence, and fear.

The economic ethic practiced among the Anabaptists is one of the clearest examples of this new social reality. From the earliest years of the Anabaptist movement in Switzerland and South Germany it is clear that concrete economic sharing was an important part of the community's life. The *Rules for Congregational Order* (1527) includes a statement on the economic practices of the community. "None of the brothers and sisters in this community should have things they call their own, but as the Christians who lived in the time of the Apostles, have everything in common and set apart a special

Edward J. Buzinski

Jan Gleysteen

(Clockwise from top left): **Peter Ediger,** Mennonite minister of Arvada, Colorado. **David Schroeder,** Mennonite Bible teacher of Winnipeg, Manitoba. **Dawn Ruth Nelson,** writer and member of the Mennonite community in Ireland. **Katie Funk Wiebe,** Mennonite Brethren author.   **José Ortiz,** Mennonite Church General Board staff secretary. **Peter J. Dyck,** Mennonite

84

Central Committee administrator. **J. B. Toews,** director of the Center for Mennonite Brethren Studies at Fresno, California. **Shantilal Bhagat,** Brethren representative at the U.N. **Anna Mow,** Church of the Brethren author and speaker. **Hubert Brown,** Mennonite minister and church administrator. **E. J. Swalm,** Brethren in Christ minister of Duntroon, Ontario.

common fund from which aid can be given to the poor, according to the needs of each. And, as in the time of the Apostles, no brother should be permitted to suffer necessity." Clearly this text indicates no common treasury for the whole congregation and its needs. Nor does it intend a revolution to abolish private property in society. However, neither did they call their property their own.

Many voluntarily shared their goods with others so that no one would suffer. Others organized themselves into communities in which goods were held in common. But, in both cases, the underlying principle was the same. In reality, the common Hutterite treasury begun in Moravia in 1528 under economic need and persecution was simply a further step in the direction already begun. To be a disciple in the community of Christ means to abandon self-centeredness in order to love and serve God and the sister and brother. Both groups were accused equally of being "revolutionaries" and "communists" because of the forms of brotherhood economics which they practiced.

We can easily see the witness of this new kind of community. A morally nonconformist community is highly visible in a generally conformist society. A community in which, contrary to all others, persons share freely with one another, lay down their lives for one another, and love even their enemies, will communicate powerfully the nature of God to the world.

Disciple Ethic

The Anabaptist vision of ethical seriousness and holiness of life in a disciple community has been described as "walking in the resurrection of Jesus Christ." The Swiss Brethren had learned from Zwingli that "to be a Christian is not to talk about Christ, but to walk as he walked." The popular motto of Hans Denk, the South German Anabaptist, is: "No one can truly know Christ except he follows him in life."

Although discipleship has become a common word in our time, its biblical meaning and practice is by no means common. Similarly, in the sixteenth century to seriously try to follow Jesus in life was something of a rarity. The established churches' attitude toward the use of arms illustrates this point. All agreed that Jesus had practiced and taught loving and sacrificial nonresistance toward violent persons. But Protestants, as well as Catholics, denied that this was intended for Christians in general. They generally held that the social order and the methods needed to conserve it had been ordained by God. Therefore it was God's will that people, even when they became Christians, should continue in their vocational callings, whatever they might be: housewife, prince, soldier, or hangman. Of course, their personal lives and worship were to be characterized by a new Christian spirit.

Their specific morals and ethics in the world continued to be determined by the natural order of things in human society. Jesus was seen as the dying Savior or the coming Judge, but rarely as Master and Lord to be concretely followed in all of life. For Anabaptists faith and obedience, as well as regeneration and discipleship, are inseparable. Because they were "born anew" the Anabaptists walked in the light of the resurrection, rather than resting in the shadow of the cross.

Missionary Community

Menno Simons described the witness of the church in the following terms: "That the name, will, Word, and ordinances of Christ are confidently confessed in the face of all cruelty, tyranny, tumult, fire, sword, and violence of the world, and sustained unto the end." Menno was not merely interested in the church's willingness to proclaim its message, but also in the context of this witness in a hostile world. In Anabaptism and the New Testament church, the two meanings of *marturia* converge. But the relationship between mission and martyrdom has been obscured in Christendom. To witness to the kingdom of God and its values is also to denounce the falsity of the other kingdom and its values.

Menno Simons was not primarily concerned about the response of the hearers to the message of the church; he was very interested in the regeneration and conversion of individuals. In this particular context he is more interested in the authenticity of the church than in assuring numerical growth. Therefore he was concerned that the authentic Christian witness be given in the face of all opposition.

In the sixteenth century, the Anabaptists found the questions dealing with the church's faith and obedience to Christ more pressing than those of evangelistic strategy. In fact, their experience led them to mistrust the large and successful movements whose influence in society was directly related to their access to power.

Thus wherever they went the Anabaptist missionaries carried their message. The Swiss Brethren defied the edicts of municipal councils and preached their radical message. Blaurock, Grebel, and Mantz in Switzerland; Reublin and Sattler in South Germany; Hut across Germany and Austria; and many more, whose names have been lost, evangelized courageously. Although some Reformers believed that the Great Commission had been fulfilled by the original apostles, the radicals of the Reformation declared that it was binding upon every member of the witnessing community.

From the viewpoint of the Anabaptists the faithfulness of the church in its mission meant persecution. Menno wrote of the "pressing cross of Christ" and insisted that this is a characteristic of the true church. Suffering is an earmark of the community which uncompromisingly commits itself to the mission of Christ. For Anabaptists suffering was not merely a result of faithfulness in personal discipleship. It was evidence of the participation of the community in the victorious struggle of Christ against the powers of this age. The Quakers would later call this "the Lamb's war," and the Brethren, "counting the cost."

Community of the Word

The Anabaptists were basically a people of the Word. In this they were not alone, for both Protestants and Catholics appealed to the Scriptures. However, the approach of the Anabaptists distinguished them from the rest. They shared with Protestantism the vision of the primacy of the Bible as the only true and reliable guide in all matters of faith. But they went beyond Luther and Zwingli in their insistence that it is also a guide in questions of practice and basic models.

In the Gospels the Anabaptists saw the "new law" of Christ presented in Jesus' example, as well as in his teachings. These guided them in all their social relationships. In the Book of Acts and the epistles they found guidelines for shaping the Christian community. Although not following the Scriptures

The discovery of the Ana-baptist tradition by radicalized evangelicals had a humbling and encouraging effect, convincing us that the questions we were raising were not unique to our generation. This was a clear sign that our task was not to construct a theology which was merely a reaction to the Vietnam war, but rather to probe biblically for what was always true about the gospel.

—Wes Michaelson

with slavish legalism, they did take the New Testament seriously as authority for *all of life*, as well as doctrine, This difference showed up most dramatically at the points where they challenged the use of violence and power: economic, social, religious, and ideological.

The Anabaptist experience clearly shows that it was not merely a question of scriptural authority, but also a matter of interpretation. The Anabaptists insisted that the Christian congregation is an interpreting community. The Swiss Brethren were no doubt indebted to Zwingli for this insight which was called the "rule of Paul," based on 1 Corinthians 14:29. The essential element in this vision consists in the gathered congregation as the place where the Scripture can be best interpreted. This approach has no special confidence in the democratic process of majority rule nor in the right of individuals to read and interpret the Scriptures for themselves. (These understandings have, however, notably influenced the way in which modern Western Protestant Christians read and interpret the Bible. This spirit has roots in the social and political thought of the past two centuries. God's people need to critically evaluate it from a biblical viewpoint.)

The New Testament vision of God's people is of an individual-in-community, participating fully with his or her gift in the life of the church. When brothers and sisters gather together in a common search for biblical solutions to their problems, the Holy Spirit is in their midst to guide them to "all truth" and make clear the meaning of Scripture (Mt. 18:20; Jn. 16:13). (The plural pronouns in both of these texts make it clear that the primary reference is to the gathered community, rather than to individuals, as such.)

The Anabaptist experience of the sixteenth century shows that this principle was not strictly limited to use in the local congregation. This vision of how the Spirit works was also applied to discernment processes in the larger brotherhood. Those who participated in the meeting at Schleitheim (1527) are examples of the Spirit's illuminating and guiding presence giving "unity" in relation to the forms that obedience should take. This experience in biblical interpretation is especially noteworthy because the consensus described in the Articles of Schleitheim was "given to them" precisely after their *dif-*

ferences had brought them together around the Word.

The Anabaptist vision of congregational biblical interpretation does not necessarily mean a rejection of the church's tradition. It simply refuses to give uncritical authority to that tradition. In relation to their contemporaries, the Anabaptists were sometimes more traditional and at other times more innovative. In contrast to the Reformers, they were "conservative" in their defense of the traditional position of the church against charging interest on loans. On the other hand, they were considered dangerous in advocating freedom of conscience which would have led to religious and social pluralism.

Conclusion

The validity of the Anabaptist vision of the church does not depend, ultimately, on its apparent relevance, but on its concrete faithfulness to its roots in Jesus and the primitive messianic community. On the other hand, to the extent that we are willing to return to our roots as God's community, we find the vision which emerges notably relevant.

The Anabaptist vision can help our churches today to the extent that we also are becoming God's community of the new covenant:

—In responding gratefully to the gracious redeeming and regenerating activity of God's Spirit.

—In being disciples according to the model of our Master and Lord.

—In experiencing the true *koinonia* of the Spirit in all social relationships.

—In conforming to Christ and thus being nonconformed to society.

—In communicating God's love both by our lives and by the gracious words by which they evangelize.

—In worship which is the joyous celebration of the kingdom which has come in Jesus and is yet to come in his second coming.

—In life sustained in the face of all odds by obedience to his Word, illuminated by his Spirit and empowered by his presence.

Such are the people of God, the community of salvation in the world.

8.
Becoming Salt and Light

Kenneth Hoover of Pennsylvania and Mahlenhle Kumalo of Zimbabwe at a celebration of the 75th anniversary of Brethren in Christ missions in Africa.

The people of God have a story which we traced from Abraham to today. They also have a mission, an agenda. The Sermon on the Mount is Jesus' agenda for his people. It was clearly the agenda of the early church. In fact, Matthew apparently intended that it be used as new membership material in the Christian movement and the early church continued this practice. And, as noted, it has been a basic agenda in all of the authentic renewal movements which have risen throughout Christian history.

Following the call to repentance (Mt. 4:17), the gathering of the discipline community (4:18-22), and the display of his messianic activity (4:23), Jesus taught his followers how to live as citizens of the kingdom of heaven. Although the teachings of Jesus are scattered throughout the four Gospels, Matthew 6 and 7 offer an essential summary of his instruction.

Jesus expected that when his disciples took these teachings seriously they would become a missionary group. The community of the Sermon on the Mount becomes a testimony to those around. They witness in being "salt and light" in their societies.

The Sermon on the Mount offers a description of life in the kingdom which Jesus began. They are not teachings for a future heavenly kingdom, as some have suggested. Jesus' intended that they direct the life and mission of God's people in the new messianic era. When this occurs the church is a witnessing community to its neighbors.

The Beatitudes describe the style of life and the values of God's people. Therefore they should not be interpreted in legalistic terms of duty and reward. The Beatitudes are not a list of activities which we can set ourselves to do through a simple act of the will. Neither should they be thought of as "counsels of perfection" which some Christians will be able to do, while others will not.

The New Testament epistles provide abundant evidence that the early church took these teachings seriously as guidelines for holy living. The similarity between these values and those described, for example, in the fruit of the Spirit in Galatians 5:22-23 is clearly evident.

The Beatitudes describe values which characterize *all*

93

members of the messianic community. They are possible for all because life in this community is lived by the grace and power of the Holy Spirit which is poured out on all God's people. The Beatitudes are an exciting description of God's grace among his people.

The Beatitudes describe realistically a concrete person, Jesus of Nazareth. They also describe the messianic community of Jesus' followers who become "salt and light" in the world. In this witness they invite others to respond in faith and obedience to God's grace.

The Sermon on the Mount declares that those who do not follow the usual values are the ones who are really "blessed." The traditional norms to determine worth, such as wealth, social position, and personal or political power, are all put aside. Even those personal achievements and possessions which are earned and defended by means of self-assertion and competitive rivalry are suspect. There is a fundamental opposition between the values of the kingdom and the value systems in society in general. This contrast underscores that the Sermon on the Mount really constitutes a frontal challenge to all other ethical systems.

This opposition is so basic that attempts to adapt or graft the principles of the Sermon on the Mount into conventional value systems run the risk of repudiating Jesus' teaching. Even so, church history is a continuous story of attempts to "put new wine into old wineskins" (Mt. 9:16, 17). In reality it is a question of the values of "the age to come" standing in opposition to those values of "the present evil age." We will explore eight of those kingdom values which witness to the world.

1. The Spirit of Poorness

This beatitude is essential for our understanding of the good news of the kingdom. It points to the character of Jesus himself, as well as to his community. In a sense, all of the Beatitudes are contained in this one. Luke's version of this beatitude clarifies the identity of these "poor" ones. "You" and "yours" clearly refer to the followers of Jesus (Lk. 6:20). These emphatic pronouns point to a specific community, to the messianic community. The Beatitudes describe the life of the people of God in contrast to all other human societies.

94

In Hebrew thought the poor person was typically a humble person. These are the ones who, in their seemingly endless experience of social and economic misery, must trust in God alone for their salvation. The Hebrew mind accentuates more the modest and humble condition of the poor than the actual absence of the necessities of life. The poor persons to whom Jesus' "good news" comes (Lk. 4:18) includes a much larger group than merely those who lack material goods. In reality, the list includes many who were considered unworthy of salvation: those of doubtful reputation and ill fame, the uncultured and the oppressed. To all these poor the gospel brought by the Messiah was genuinely saving news.

In Western Christianity a widely held understanding views the gospel as an instrument which promotes upward social and economic mobility. The gospel when preached to the poor will most certainly lead to prosperity, it is claimed. But this common view among evangelical Christians can easily become a shamefully twisted version of the gospel of Jesus Christ. The social and economic mobility to which Jesus calls us is *toward the poor* (Rom. 12:16). The gospel is a call to orient our lives according to the spirit of Jesus who "emptied himself taking the form of a servant" (Phil. 2:5-8).

Of course, some in the Christian church have tended to glorify poverty as a value in and of itself. Jesus expects his disciples to have detachment from, and generosity with, material wealth. Material goods should be used in the service of humanity, rather than being allowed to exercise control over us. The people of God will engage in productive occupations, but not to enrich themselves personally. They will work in order to contribute to the welfare of others (Eph. 4:28).

2. Sorrow

The second beatitude, as well as the rest, does not designate a new category of persons, but rather describes more fully those who have already been identified as "poor." All of the Beatitudes describe the new messianic community of believer-disciples. "Those who mourn," in the Greek text (present participle), describes the character, or the essential nature, of God's people. They are not melancholy persons or chronic criers, but persons who are deeply concerned.

95

*Christum vermag niemand
dass er Ihm nachfolge im L*

*No one can truly know
except he follows him i*

Authentic repentance, which is required for entrance into the kingdom, involves a radical reorientation toward life and a change of values. It places one in direct conflict with the values of a fallen world. This fundamental opposition of values and lifestyles will bring affliction which is both subjective (deep concern for others) and objective (the pain which results from persecution).

These people do not feel good about things as they are in the world. They are not happy with the present value system nor with the forms of human relations in society. But it is not merely a question of inner suffering of the spirit. It is also real suffering coming as a result of opposition and persecution. Only those who are uncomfortable with the values of the present age and who through repentance have radically changed their lives will experience the true consolation of the messianic kingdom.

3. Meekness

The third beatitude appears to be a direct reference to Psalm 37:11. The context within which this phrase is set in the

ahrlich zu erkennen, es sei denn
en.

hrist,
fe.

— Hans Denck

psalm will help us to understand its meaning here in the Sermon on the Mount. The meek person is powerless and non-violent, trusting in God, placing hope in him. The meek one is just and merciful. Poor and humble, the meek one has no other alternative than to depend on God for survival.

In Psalm 37 this is the person who is contrasted with the wicked, the wrongdoers, the one who carries out evil devices and plots against the righteous, the one who works against the poor and needy, the violent one. The meek person is characterized by concern for justice and peace and whose survival ultimately depends upon a God who is just and loving.

In Psalm 37 God graciously gives the promised land to the meek and the humble. Here Jesus offers the "promised land" of the kingdom to the meek and the humble. In his Gospel, Luke describes how the kingdom will be given through the grace of God to his people. "Instead, seek his kingdom, and these things shall be yours as well. Fear not, little flock, for it is your Father's good pleasure to give you the kingdom" (Lk. 12:31-32).

97

According to the biblical vision, the true meaning of history flows through the channel of God's kingdom. When human history ends, the meek of God, together with their meek and humble Lord, will prevail rather than violent and self-seeking persons. We should not be deceived. Those who appear to be great and powerful upon the earth will not have the last word, in spite of all appearances to the contrary.

In their meekness the citizens of the kingdom are simply anticipating the time when that kingdom comes in all of its fullness. "The Lamb that was slain," the meek and lowly one, will be manifested as "Lord of lords." This is a patient confidence in the One who will be the champion of the humiliated. It is not like the attitude of the Zealots who waged guerrilla warfare or the Essenes of Qumram, who predicted the coming of a holy war in which they would be participants.

The triumphant confidence of the meek is also different from the utter subjection of oppressed peoples who live without any real hope. The meek are those who dare to live in hope as they seek to incarnate the new alternative of the kingdom.

4. Justice

This beatitude pictures the urgent desire of the people of God for justice. People who suffer hunger, and above all, thirst, are those who find themselves at the very limits of their resistance. Although, in his version, Luke does not add the word "righteousness" (6:21), surely his meaning is similar to Matthew's. After all, the blessings of the messianic kingdom are not limited to bread (although they most certainly include it). They include the entire range of right and just social relationships which characterize "righteousness" in Hebrew thought.

The prophetic understanding of righteousness or justice is practically the same as peace and salvation (Is. 51:5-8; 52:7). It includes that wide range of virtues which contribute to relationships among persons, and between persons and God, which are right and whole (healed). In short, righteousness describes the quality of relationships which characterizes life among the people of God. In Matthew righteousness often means a good relationship with God which is experienced by submitting to his will with all of its social and economic consequence. Clearly in the Sermon on the Mount, God's will implies ordering one's life according to the values in Jesus' teachings. So righteousness has to do with just relationships among persons, as well as between God and people.

5. Mercy

Matthew uses this term to mean to pardon the offenses of others (9:13; 12:7; 18:33; 23:23), as well as to do good to all who are needy (9:27; 15:22; 20:30, 31). God's people are known for their readiness to forgive the sins of others, as well as by their willingness to contribute to the well-being of anyone who may be in need.

The messianic community is the place in which forgiveness is experienced. The forgiveness of God becomes a reality which is communicated through brothers and sisters within his family (Mt. 18:15-20). The meaning of this beatitude is illustrated in the parable of the unmerciful servant (Mt. 18:21-35).

In addition to the forgiveness of sins experienced in the messianic community, other works of mercy also flourish. These expressions of mercy contribute to the healing, well-being, and salvation of brothers and sisters in the family of God.

6. Sincerity

The sixth beatitude describes persons who are sincere, whose loyalty is undivided, whose morality is marked by integrity. The man described in Psalm 24:4 is a good example of the virtue described in this beatitude: "He who has clean hands and a pure heart, who does not lift up his soul to what is false, and does not swear deceitfully." It refers to sincerity, to openness of intention and character, to purity of purpose.

The integrity of the people of God stands in sharp contrast to the hypocrisy which Jesus condemned among the people of his time. A hypocrite was originally an actor in ancient Greek theater who wore a mask in the presentation of his role. Among God's people masks must be removed. Participation in the kingdom requires genuine repentance which permits us to be sincere and open before God as well as in the presence of our brothers and sisters. A person who is not sincere with the church will hardly be sincere with God, nor with self.

ff your first thought of role?
or outline on passive

7. Peacemakers

Of all the Beatitudes, this one has probably been most misunderstood by the Christian church throughout its history. Perhaps the Latin Vulgate translation, "beati pacifici" has contributed to this misunderstanding. In reality, "pacifici" are peacemakers, which expresses quite well the meaning of the Greek term. However, in the life of the church this beatitude has come to mean peaceful persons, those who are pacific, or, at best, pacifiers.

This meaning is a far cry from the "creators of shalom" which Jesus had in mind. By definition, the peacemaker is an activist. He creates peace. Rather than making destruction, he, like God, loves his enemies, making peace and reconciliation live possibilities. Peacemakers are those who contribute joyfully and hopefully to that peace, justice, and salvation of the messianic kingdom.

Shalom was a fundamental idea among the Hebrews. It meant well-being, health, and salvation in its fullest sense, both material and spiritual. It described the situation of well-being which resulted from truly whole (healed) relationships among persons, as well as between persons and God.

According to the Old Testament prophets, shalom reigned in Israel when there was social justice. Shalom was when the cause of the poor and the weak was heard, when equal opportunity was given to all, in short, when the people enjoyed salvation according to the intention of God's covenant. On the other hand, when there were injustices and suffering caused by social and economic oppression, there was no shalom.

In reality, peacemakers who dedicate themselves to creating God's shalom are participants in his mission. Peacemakers bear a very special relationship to the "God of peace." In the kingdom begun by Jesus, peacemakers will be recognized as "sons of God." God is the peacemaker par excellence who creates his shalom among people, doing good to all equally, loving even his enemies. Rather than merely being peaceful or serene persons, peacemakers are God's activists engaged in the task of healing in a broken world.

8. Suffering

The last beatitude points out that the people of God who live the first seven are persecuted. The tense of the verb "are persecuted"—indicates that it is the result of an earlier situation. Citizens of Jesus' kingdom suffer persecution by the world because their radically different values cannot be tolerated. In reality, the persecution of God's people gives testimony that the values of Jesus' disciples are inspired by a different Spirit.

The "you" pronouns in verses 11 and 12 mean that these words are directed to the entire messianic community. The world's verdict on the life and work of Jesus was the cross. In the same way, the world's verdict on kingdom values is the reviling and the persecution which Jesus' community suffers. In the messianic community this suffering is borne with joy because it simply identifies them as true disciples of Jesus (1 Pet. 4:13, 14).

Verse 12 reminds God's people that their sufferings are neither new, nor accidental, nor absurd. They are charged with significance when viewed from the perspective of the history of salvation. The story of God's people shows that his true witnesses have always suffered at the hands of evil persons. This kind of suffering identifies the people of God as true followers of the Messiah.

The values of the messianic community run counter to those in fallen society. Jesus' disciples bear with joy this continuous source of conflict and suffering. God's people are lifted up by the confident assurance that they are indeed witnesses of the future. The values of the community of the Messiah are sure signs of the kingdom inaugurated by Jesus which one day will break forth in all of its fullness. This reality, anchored in the ancient promises of God and clearly revealed in Jesus, fills with meaning the hope of God's people.

Salt and Light

Salt and light are images which describe the witness of God's community. The essential relationship between these figures and the preceding paragraph is highlighted by the use of the plural pronoun "you," first in verses 11 and 12, and now in verses 13 and 14. In the Greek text "you" is given special emphasis, both by its grammatical form and by its position in the sentence. It is as if Jesus had said: "Blessed are *you* as hearers of my words and participants in my kingdom. It is for this reason that *you* are being persecuted. But it is precisely *you* who are the salt of the earth and the light of the world."

In the New Testament it is no accident that the same term applies to both martyr and witness. The suffering and testimony of God's people are two sides of the same coin. The suffering community gathered by the suffering Messiah will be salt in the earth and light in the world through the character of its life and works which correspond to the kingdom.

The verbs in verses 13 and 14 are often overlooked in the interpretation of these verses. They show that Jesus does not command his disciples to be salt and light. He simply declares that the community described in the foregoing Beatitudes is, by the very nature of things, salt and light. There are no evangelism techniques for becoming salt and light independently of the values and styles of life described in the Sermon on the Mount.

Conclusion

In his use of the image of light, Jesus notes the missionary visibility of the people of God. The community of the beatitudes which carries on the work of Jesus will be light for the world. The result of this highly visible testimony, which includes the entire life and activity of the messianic community, will be the glory of God. This glorification of the God of Israel by all peoples and nations was one of the clearest characteristics of the messianic era according to Jewish expectations.

The holiness of life and works of God's people are the clearest testimony that God has truly come in human history and that his reign is a reality. The best contribution which the people of God can make to society is that of lives and works which already participate in the "age to come." They contribute lives which manifest those relationships of the kingdom of God. By their form of being, doing, and saying, they proclaim the kingdom. They become God's saving action in the world.

9.
Called to a
Higher Righteousness

Jesus offers radical new approaches to problems which resisted solution when they were tackled in traditional ways. These problems include anger (Mt. 5:21-26), marital infidelity (27-30), divorce (31-32), falsehood (33-37), vengeance (38-42), and hatred toward one's enemies (43-48). In each case his statement is negative, in that the problem, as such, is taken as the point of discussion.

Here, as in the Ten Commandments, we find solutions to attitudes and actions which have no place in the life of the people of God. However, in their impact, the teachings of Jesus are positive because they point toward a life characterized by peace, respect for one another and mutual confidence, trustworthiness, truthfulness, redemptive attitudes toward offenders, and love toward all, even those who are enemies. This is the higher righteousness to which Jesus calls the people of God.

God's Law and the Mission of the Messiah (Mt. 5:17-20)

Jesus' attitude toward the law has two aspects. First, although he condemned the legalistic misunderstandings of his time, Jesus insisted that it was his mission to carry forward God's law. Second, he carried God's covenant intention for the life of his people to its fullest expression. Matthew probably included the observations in verses 17-20 on the function of

103

law in the messianic era in order to correct some sort of misunderstanding. The term translated "think" in verse 17 is also used in this sense of correcting in Matthew 10:34 and 20:10.

Jesus rejected the idea that his messianic mission was to lead God's people away from the authentic authority of his covenant. On the contrary, God has commissioned Jesus to "give fullness" to the "law and the prophets." As Messiah, Jesus is the new Moses, lawgiver par excellence.

For Jesus the understanding of covenant law was as natural as his proclamation of the gospel of the kingdom. As Messiah, Jesus understood God's law as the expression of his intention for the life of people. Therefore Jesus offers his teachings as the fulfillment and full flowering of God's covenant intention. Jesus deepens the understanding of law commonly held by discerning its essential spirit and its radical intent. In this Jesus fulfills his messianic function. The Jews looked forward, in their messianic expectation, to the last times when there would be an authoritative and definitive interpretation of the law of God. In reality Jesus was the full revelation of God's intention for his people.

The Problem of Anger (Mt. 5:21-26)

The phrase, "you have heard that it was said to men of old," is probably a reference to the traditional teachings which the first-century Jews received in their synagogues. Verse 21 is a clear reference to the sixth commandment of the Decalogue in which murder was absolutely forbidden.

"But I say to you" (22) introduces the original understanding which Jesus gives to this commandment. Its fulfillment goes to the very root of God's intention for life together in the covenant community. The use of the term "brother" four times in verses 22 to 24 indicates that Jesus is dealing with interpersonal relationships in the messianic community. The disciples of Jesus not only do not commit homicide, they also refrain from all expressions of anger which destroy their brothers and sisters. Jesus understood very well that anger is the seed that can lead to murder when it matures. And anger in all of its forms leads to the destruction of integrity in interpersonal relationships. Wrath destroys community.

104

The three representative expressions of wrath mentioned in Matthew 5:22 are apparently meant to be understood in terms of increasing seriousness.

1. "Every one who is angry with his brother shall be liable to judgment" seems to mean that, in seriousness, nursing anger toward another needs to be evaluated in the same way that murder was judged under traditional structures. Passion which may ripen into murder is the root of murder and should be dealt with just as seriously as the killing itself. In this way Jesus restates the old law, placing it on a higher level which more fully expresses God's intention. The verb translated "is angry" is the same term used in that seemingly strange text found in Ephesians 4:26 (RSV), "Be angry, but do not sin." Here the verb can be indicative, as well as imperative, and is probably better translated in the *New English Bible*, "If you are angry, do not let anger lead you into sin; do not let sunset find you still nursing it; leave no loophole for the devil."

2. "Whoever insults his brother shall be liable to the council." In this case "council" probably refers to the Sanhedrin, a first-century supreme court in Judaism. The term of abuse here translated "insults" is really the word "raca" and means something like imbecile, or crazy, or stupid. Anger which is not only harbored but nurtured by insulting attitudes

Matthew 5:17-21

"Think not that I have come to abolish the law and the prophets; I have come not to abolish them but to fulfil them. For truly, I say to you, till heaven and earth pass away, not an iota, not a dot, will pass from the law until all is accomplished. Whoever then relaxes one of the least of these commandments and teaches men so, shall be called least in the kingdom of heaven; but he who does them and teaches them shall be called great in the kingdom of heaven. For I tell you, unless your righteousness exceeds that of the scribes and Pharisees, you will never enter the kingdom of heaven."

and words is even more dangerous and deserves even more serious treatment.

3. "Whoever says, 'You fool!' shall be liable to the hell of fire." This is literally "the Gehenna of fire," a ravine on the edge of Jerusalem in which the sacrifices to Molech were offered in earlier days. This ravine became a symbol of judgment and perdition. The term translated "fool" was an extremely serious insult among the Jews. It amounted to calling one a "renegade" which in effect meant cutting him or her off from the people of God. This is the final stage of the process which begins with anger and is nurtured with insults. To be cut off from the people of God was in effect to be condemned to death.

All of these degrees of intensity, attitudes, and expressions which harm the brother or sister are forbidden in the community of the Messiah. Although the Christian church, as well as ancient Israel, consistently opposed homicide in its literal form, its defense of Jesus' teaching has not been clear.

We tend to overlook many destructive forms of anger in social relationships. Popular psychology encourages people to "get their feelings out," to express anger for the sake of one's emotional health, sometimes without regard for the destructive impact anger may have on others. Jesus' words forbid this lack of concern for brothers and sisters.

On the other hand, Christians may be tempted to deny anger. Jesus wants his disciples to be free from anger, not to deny it. Other passages indicate that when anger and hate feelings crop up, they should be dealt with immediately, before they hurt and become unmanageable.

The community of Jesus Christ has alternate ways to help the spiritual and emotional health of its members. It handles anger honestly and responsibly, rather than with damaging outbursts and insults. The need for self-expression and emotional release is subordinate to concern for the salvation of brothers and sisters.

In order to keep anger and its bitter fruits from taking root in his community, Jesus gives two practical alternate suggestions in Matthew 5:24 and 25:

1. "First be reconciled to your brother." As soon as persons become conscious that they have committed an offense, they

should take the initiative to become reconciled with the offended one. This may mean even interrupting worship at its highest moment. True worship is possible only within a community of reconciled brothers and sisters. For a Jew, worship is the highest and holiest action a person can perform. But even worship is dependent upon restored relationships.

2. "Make friends quickly with your accuser." Personal offenses should be clarified, confessed, and forgiven regularly and without delay. This really is the original meaning of the verb "make friends." Taking the initiative immediately in reconciliation may avoid situations which develop when offenses degenerate into attitudes of hate and outright conflict. This approach also protects the offended brother or sister against the temptation to become angry at the offender. (Note also similar counsel by Paul in Ephesians 4:26b, 27.)

The Problem of Marital Infidelity (Mt. 5:27-30)

In verse 27 Jesus refers to the seventh commandment which forbids adultery. Not surprisingly, two of the six representative problems which Matthew has included in this collection of Jesus' teachings deal with relationships between the sexes (adultery and divorce). This was a matter of great concern among the Jews of the first century. Furthermore, it represented one of the principal points of ethical conflict between Judaic Christianity and Greco-Roman culture.

In his return to original intentions, Jesus used the tenth commandment to show that coveting the neighbor's wife, in effect, already makes one an adulterer. By pointing out that adultery already exists in the act of coveting the neighbor's wife, Jesus defines the problem in basic Hebrew concepts. Adultery is not merely a matter of personal sexual purity, as dualistic Greek thinking considered the problem, but rather an act which affects the well-being of another person—the neighbor. Disciples of Jesus do not only avoid temptations to marital unfaithfulness in order to maintain their own purity; rather, they are motivated with a concern for the well-being of the other person.

The teaching of Jesus, as well as the references from the Ten Commandments, are directed to men in their relationships with married women. Undoubtedly this way of stating the prob-

107

A person
who rejects God's
government is
condemned to live
under the tyranny
of self.

—William Penn

lem is due to the patriarchal social organization in ancient Israel and first-century Judaism. Under this system a woman's social life was determined by a man, her father or her husband.

Certainly in the social organization of modern Western society, the words of Jesus would also be directed to women. Today both women and men can legally divorce and either has the power to harm or destroy the conjugal union of others. To these relationships Jesus brings a clear word: harm not the other's union. Recognizing the power of temptation, Jesus goes to the root of the issue to offer the solution.

Verse 28 does not refer to a glance of admiration or the beauty of body as described in the Hebrews' Song of Songs. Rather, Jesus is referring to a covetous and lustful look. As in the case of killing, Jesus shows that the root of the offense lies in the intention. Therefore to look at a person with lascivious desire is to be an adulterer. But the physical dimensions of the problem are not ignored. Jesus was concretely interested in the way in which the body reflects the person's intention.

Verses 29 and 30 should not be dismissed as mere Hebrew hyperbole (overstatement). They remind us how important the members of our bodies are for us to function as persons. Although sin is capable of controlling the heart and mind, the body's members become sin's immediate instruments. Plucking out one's eye would not guarantee victory over the inner springs of adultery. Instead Jesus asks that the body's members respond to the sound impulses of the heart in the best interests of the neighbor, rather than opening themselves to evil.

The profound concern of Jesus for the total person is clear in these verses. Jesus is not merely interested in the soul, or the heart, but also the body. The body is beautiful and important. Sexuality is a precious and joyful gift to humanity. As with other gifts of God, Jesus teaches us to care for them in our concrete social relationships. It is a very serious thing to harm one's neighbor!

The Problem of Divorce (Mt. 5:32-32)

Jesus here refers to the Mosaic provision designed to protect a woman who has been repudiated by her husband

109

(Deut. 24:1). Here, as in the preceding paragraph, Jesus' purpose is to defend the integrity of marriage: there against marital infidelity and here, against divorce. In first-century Judaism one theological school interpreted the Mosaic legislation in its most liberal sense. Over against this school, the teaching of Jesus defends the kingdom ideal that marriage is not to be dissolved.

Jesus, in the best prophetic tradition (Mal. 2:14-16), insists on the sacred character of the marriage covenant as the true intention of God for the life of his people. Jesus' teaching on divorce is not a code to regulate public morality. Legislation which merely imposes formal monogamy is unable to enforce marital fidelity, and is therefore not a real solution to the problem. The Sermon on the Mount reflects an ethic of grace and is intended for disciples of Jesus in the context of the messianic community.

These teachings of Jesus which deal with the marital relationships of men and women are also highly relevant for the life of God's people today. In the face of the rapid disintegration of marriage and the nuclear family—a genuine threat in an already fragmented world—the teachings of Jesus are a clear defense of innocent children, as well as men and women who so easily fall prey to the selfish designs of others. In a society oriented toward the perverted exploitation of sex for selfish purposes, Jesus would have us show concern for the well-being of the neighbor.

We should remember that all basically selfish perversions of sex carry within themselves the seeds of destruction. Pornography, for example, which encourages sexual gratification in the unreal and imaginary world of fantasy proves in the end to be frustrating and destructive. Sexual practices which are oriented exclusively to satisfy the self-centered impulses of the individual deny, in reality, the basically social functions of sex. These, too, prove to be illusory. The promiscuous relationships in liberal Western societies make a mockery of the true realization of personhood so desperately sought.

All these and other basically selfish perversions of sex run contrary to the best counsels of our history: the witness of ancient Israel (Deut. 22:22), the practice and teachings of Jesus (Mt. 15:19), the teachings of the early church (1 Cor. 6:9;

Gal. 5:18; Eph. 5:3, 5), and the experience of human societies in general. They do not contribute to true personal well-being nor to authentically satisfying social relationships.

We live in a culture which overrates the experience of intercourse and exaggerates its importance for self-expression, fulfillment, and meeting physical need. Our society finds it hard to conceive of celibacy as a serious option for healthy people. In this context Jesus' disciples face a real challenge to demonstrate that affectionate, familial relationships within the messianic community contribute far more to personal and corporate well-being than promiscuous encounters. In such a community the contributions, needs, and potential for wholeness of all people, single and married, can be recognized. The Christian community replaces the exaggerated attention to erotic love and sex with an appreciation of celibacy as well as appreciation for intercourse within permanent, lifelong covenant.

Modern Western Christians generally seek more social and spiritual security in the biological family than in the family of God. But in reality, the nuclear family is often little more than the extension of individual selfishness. Social families made up by people of a race, nation, or ethnic group also often feed on self-interest. In this context the community of the Messiah witnesses that God has acted in human history to create a new social reality, the family of God. This family gathers up and transcends the possibilities for human well-being found in the biological family or other social families. Here true salvation is experienced. Here self-centered individualism, clannish tribalism, and proud nationalism are overcome. Here we find true life in laying down our lives for one another (Mt. 10:37-39).

The Problem of Falsehood (Mt. 5:33-37)

Jesus radicalizes the ancient law forbidding the swearing of false oaths by pointing out that it is God's intention that persons always be truthful. In fact, this eliminates the need for swearing oaths. Truthfulness is assured, not through the external means of an oath, but through the inner honesty of the person. The oath, by its very nature, implies the dishonest character of the person who swears and an essential lack of trust in the one who accepts the oath. Therefore in the

Connie Isaac, Mennonite Brethren folk singer.

messianic community where evil in general, and dishonesty in particular, are rejected, the oath is out of place.

According to Jesus, all oaths are wrong in the messianic community where interpersonal relationships are characterized by sincerity. "Yes" means yes and "no" means no (Jas. 5:12). In the community of Christ all superfluous words are out of place. In the body of Christ words take on their full meaning and language is used with sobriety. Communication is employed with modesty in the interests of the common good (Jas. 3:1-12).

Only within the community of the Messiah can unchecked communication be stripped of demonic power and unmasked as the giant evil that it has become. In the Christian community, language is simple and unostentatious. The truth is spoken. In fact, Jesus warns that "anything more than this comes from [the] evil [one]." This is probably a reference to Satan, "the father of lies," but it also warns us of the demonic power of propaganda in our world. Due to the untruthful nature of many relationships in society, the oath has become a "necessity" in public life. But in the messianic community simple, sincere, truthful communication makes the oath obsolete.

Falsehood and deceit, on one hand, and transparent sincerity, on the other, characterize two kingdoms which are fundamentally opposed. Even though truthfulness is a rare virtue in society, in Jesus' community disciples are to be sincere. However, this does not mean that we are free to be brutal in our candor, or cruel in our concern for the truth. Among the followers of Jesus the truth is spoken in love (Eph. 4:15).

Conclusion

These four examples of problem areas in human relationships remind us of the many moral compromises which infect all humanity and our social structures. On the other hand, these problems furnish Jesus the occasion to present breathtaking glimpses of the possibilities open to the community whose life is empowered by his Spirit. In his life and teachings Jesus shows clearly that the agenda of God's people is to practice that higher righteousness. It exceeds all human possibilities and reflects the true intention of God.

10.
Practicing
Nonresistant Love

In a day when the very existence of the world and humanity is threatened by a nuclear holocaust, humanity's rebellion expresses itself principally in self-centered violence. This rebellion is especially evident today. God's answer is a new humanity. God's response to the confusion and futility of fallen human enterprise at Babel was the formation of a people oriented in the "name" (or character) of God. Furthermore, the prophetic vision saw in the coming Messiah and his people an era of peace in which the vicarious suffering of God's Servant (and servant people) is the path to reconciliation. We must view the life and mission of the people of the new covenant from this viewpoint.

Therefore, the nonresistant self-giving love of the church of Jesus Christ is not legalistically based on a series of scattered proof texts, such as those found in this section of the Sermon on the Mount or in Romans 12. On the contrary, these New Testament texts simply show that the messianic community saw in the self-sacrificing love of Jesus the clearest and highest revelation of God's essential character. Just as the people of God in the old covenant were those who reflected the character of God, so the messianic community of the new covenant is the vehicle of the Spirit.

Surely it is not by chance that God's answer to a violent and rebellious humanity is a community of love and peace. In the same way that human violence is expressed in social dimensions, God's alternative is also social—a community of peace. This radical answer to human rebellion is really a return to God's primary intention expressed first in creation and then renewed and transcended in His new creation. Peoplehood is essential in God's program. God wants agape love and shalom peace to be expressed socially in the life and witness of his people. The function of this community is not merely to serve as a springboard from which individual peacemakers are launched into the world to fulfill their mission. Although heroic individuals are sometimes capable of inspiring admiration, only in the messianic community of self-sacrificing and vicarious love do we find the resources capable of overcoming humanity's rebellion and violence.

Jesus' teaching in the Sermon on the Mount on vengeance and violence toward the enemy must be approached from this viewpoint. Because God, as revealed so clearly in Jesus, is characterized by self-giving unconditional love, these teachings find their authority in the very nature of God. Furthermore, they assume the community of the new creation where evil is overcome, in the Spirit of Jesus, by this same self-giving love.

God's answer to human violence is the community of peace. We are not dealing with a theme which is secondary to the task of the church. Nonresistant love has to do with the very essence of the gospel.

The Problem of Vengeance (Mt. 5:38-42)

This problem is the fifth example which Jesus used to describe the higher righteousness which his kingdom community practices. Jesus reminded his followers that another of the Old Testament teachings which the rabbis had been repeating in the synagogues was the so-called "law of talion" (Lev. 24:20). This principle held that relatiation should be limited to being like the offense. In popular instruction it meant simply "an eye for an eye and a tooth for a tooth" (Ex. 21:24; Lev. 24:20; Deut. 19:20).

Although the rigor of this Old Testament punishment is sometimes underscored, we should remember that this provision was a notable improvement over the anarchic system of unrestricted personal vengeance. For example, Lamech's practically unlimited desire for vengeance had little relation to the original offense (Gen. 4:23, 24). In reality, the talion principle was designed to protect the offender against disproportionate retaliation. It was an ancient attempt to keep the spiral of violence under control.

But even to this advanced principle Jesus says to his disciples, "Do not resist one who is evil" (Mt. 5:39). With this statement Jesus moves beyond all other positions before him, in regards to evildoers. Perhaps an exception may be found in some of the ideas found in the Suffering Servant Songs of Isaiah (e.g., chapter 53). Exhortations to be patient toward others and to practice mutual aid were well known in Judaism. However, Jesus' total condemnation of legal action and retaliation and his willingness to suffer unjustly rather than to inflict suffering were totally unknown.

Some have said that the ethic which we find in the Sermon on the Mount is strictly individual. Some would further claim that to develop a social ethic capable of restraining evil human impulses, it is necessary to fall back on the law of talion. In reality, it is not a matter of a personal ethic (the Sermon on the Mount) in opposition to a social or collective ethic (the law of talion). Here the new morality of the kingdom, which is both individual and collective, is contrasted with the ethic of the established social order. The old order, in reality, participates in "this present evil age" and is therefore destined to pass away.

To "not resist one who is evil" in reality means that a person will love and do good to the evildoer, even though one steadfastly opposes evil. To not resist one who is evil and not respond to evil persons with violence or a spirit of retaliation was so novel and so revolutionary that Jesus found it necessary to employ four examples to illustrate the principle.

These four concrete examples should not be understood as rules in a legalistic sense, but rather as examples of ways to apply Jesus' principle. Jesus' hearers might experience these practical examples, but they certainly do not exhaust the meaning or the consequences of the principle, "Do not resist one who is evil."

(1.) The first of these examples is drawn from the field of interpersonal relationships. "But if any one strikes you on the right cheek, turn to him the other also" (Mt. 5:39b). To strike a person on the cheek with the back of one's hand (in this case a right-handed person would necessarily tap the other person on his *right* cheek) constituted a most offensive form of insulting another person in the ancient world. In fact, this is still the case in the Near East.

In the blow here described, the problem is not so much a matter of physical harm, but rather the humiliating insult which one has received. Jesus teaches that his disciples should accept one insult after another without returning the affront. Such a response corresponds exactly with the prophetic vision of the Suffering Servant of Yahweh (Is. 50:6) and to the attitude which Jesus himself later showed (Mt. 26:67; Mk. 14:65).

2. The second example is drawn from the field of legal relationships. "If anyone would sue you and take your coat, let him have your cloak as well" (Mt. 5:40). Here Jesus is saying that his disciples will not respond violently to persons who demand something which does not belong to them. In fact, they will treat their enemy with generosity.

This is not an idealistic ethic which was therefore never attempted in the primitive community. Although the rabbinic tradition points out that a craze for lawsuits existed in Palestine in Jesus' time, the attitude of the apostles on this matter was clear. Paul's instructions to the church in Corinth show that he had understood perfectly well the Spirit of Jesus (1 Cor. 6:7, 8). Living in the midst of Hellenistic society in which legal action was a common practice, Paul warns that it is better to suffer wrong, and even to be defrauded, than to sue one's neighbor even with just cause. In Jesus' example there is no question that justice would have been on the side of the disciple, since the law protected the poor and forbade despoiling him of his garment (Ex. 22:25 f.; Deut. 24:12 f.).

3. The third example is taken from political relationships. "If any one forces you to go one mile, go with him two miles" (Mt. 5:41). In this case Jesus is referring to the right of government officials to exact forced labor from their subjects. In the time of Jesus, Palestine was a colony within the Roman Empire. Imperial officials and soldiers in the occupation forces could require any passerby to carry their baggage, or to accompany them as a hostage or a guide.

Ruth Minter and Michele Baldwin at a Brethren in Christ learning center in the Bronx, New York.

118

It is not difficult to imagine what the attitude of the Jews in general toward these representatives of an oppressive foreign regime must have been. For this reason, this example is all the more noteworthy, indeed, daring.

Jesus says that his disciples will render the services which are required: in fact, they will even go beyond that which is imposed. In no sense do they do this in order to express their approval of the injustices which were committed by the oppressors. Neither were they helping in the oppression. Rather, this was a concrete expression of concern for the well-being of that particular person who required their help, even though he was a hated member of the foreign legion or a Roman official. Here was a concrete way of responding to the violence of oppression with genuine goodness and loving concern for the other person. It was a way of breaking the spiral of violence.

4. The fourth example is taken from the field of economic relationships. "Give to him who begs from you, and do not refuse him who would borrow from you" (Mt. 5:42). The context would lead us to imagine that this "begging" and "borrowing" has to do with a somewhat violent demand which is not based on the legitimate claim of the person who insists. This is the idea which one gets from Luke's parallel: "Give to everyone who asks you, and do not ask for your property back from the man who robs you" (6:30, *The Jerusalem Bible*). In this context verse 42 does not call so much for an act of mutual aid or of brotherly love, as it does a gesture of peacemaking and an attitude of patience in response to the violence to another. The virtues of the disciples of Jesus here are generosity, good will, and patience.

Jesus offers four examples of what the application of a spirit free from vengeance might mean in the disciples' daily lives. Certainly other situations could also be named. This spirit of Jesus and his disciples has the power to transform interpersonal relationships. Paul caught this intention of Jesus in his writing to the Christians in Rome, "Do not be overcome by evil, but overcome evil with good" (Rom. 12:21).

Above all, we should remember that this is the way God has responded to a rebellious world in the person of his Messiah. God adopted this strategy to break the spiral of violence in its most vicious form.

The Problem of Hatred Toward Enemies
(Mt. 5:43-48)

In the sixth of these representative instructions included in the Sermon on the Mount Jesus reminds his disciples that they have been taught to love their neighbors and to hate their enemies (Mt. 5:43). The command to love one's neighbor was well known in the Old Testament (Lev. 19:18) and it formed a part of Jesus' summary of "all the law and the prophets" (Mt. 22:37-40). However the second part of this traditional teaching, "hate your enemy," is not found anywhere in the Old Testament, at least not explicitly.

This phrase may have entered in religious instruction among the Jews because all those who did not belong to the national and religious community of the Jews were, in fact, considered to be enemies of God and his people. This fact justified the "holy hatred" of God's people. In fact, this hatred does not seem so much to be personal and passionate, as it does collective and religious. In the context of Matthew, it appears to be a natural response to persecution (Mt. 5:44; 10:22; 24:9).

But an even clearer explanation can probably be found in the attitude of the Essene community toward its enemies. In many ways the Essenes were like Jesus in their approach to the law. They were serious in their insistence on obedience to its demands. They were also radically serious in their application of the Old Testament Scriptures.

But the Essenes' understanding of the nature of God led them to form a closed community which demanded hatred of those outside. At this point Jesus and his community differed sharply from the Essenes. This reference to hatred of enemies may well have been a direct allusion to the Essenes.

Jesus radicalizes the law which calls on persons to love their neighbors by extending it to include enemies. Furthermore, this love of Jesus is not merely the absence of hatred and vengeance. Consistent with biblical thought, Jesus expects this love to be shown in action. Jesus charges his disciples to pray for their persecutors (Mt. 5:44) and to greet their enemies as well as their friends (Mt. 5:47). But above all, the heavenly Father who "makes his sun rise on the evil and the good, and sends rain on the just and on the unjust" (Mt. 5:45)

The regenerated
do not go to war,
nor engage in strife.
They are the children of peace
who have beaten their swords
into plowshares and their spears
into pruning hooks,
and know of no war.

– Menno Simons

best shows the kind of love which Jesus expects of his followers.

In order to be in fact, what they are in principle—children of God—Jesus calls on his disciples to love in the same way in which God loves. Although even pagans are capable of certain expressions of love which are motivated by their own self-interest, children of God are to love just as God loves, unselfishly and even self-sacrificially, without questioning the worthiness of those who are the objects of his love (see Lk. 6:34, 35).

"You, therefore, must be perfect, as your heavenly Father is perfect" (Mt. 5:48) is both a promise and a command. The disciples of the Messiah are to imitate their Father (as well as the Son) in the indiscriminating way in which they love. The people of God should resemble God in his way of loving. This text does not teach Christian perfectionism in some abstract or philosophical sense. Jesus is simply pointing out that the love of the disciples will be complete, mature, or perfect, when it resembles the lavish and indiscriminate love of God.

In the parallel passage in Luke, Jesus calls on his disciples to "be merciful, even as your Father is merciful" (6:36). The term "perfect," in this text, probably reflects the Hebrew concept of "wholeness" or "integrity." God has always expected integrity of his people (Deut. 18:13). This is the nature of perfection rather than, as often interpreted, a human striving after faultlessness. Love for one's enemies is an essential part of Christian living which insures its integrity. In fact, this love is the fundamental difference which distinguishes it from all other "ethics."

In every sphere of human relationships one observes the prominent role of "enmity" as a principle of social organization. Political alignments in international relations seem to be oriented around the principles of ideological, socio-political, and economic competition. In interpersonal relationships, an enormous amount of energy is dedicated to competing with others. It almost seems as if we need someone against whom we can struggle.

This tendency toward hostility is found in family relationships, neighborhoods, relationships between labor and management, and, we might as well admit it, Christian congregations. The struggles which divide us in the church are not generally based on real concerns about maintaining sound doctrine or genuine ethical considerations. They are, rather, hostilities which are the products of personal self-interest.

But life in the messianic community will be different. God's people will find concrete ways to show love toward their enemies and to seek their well-being. They do not practice the way of love for pragmatic reasons, but simply because this is the way in which God acts.

This spirit of love, which refuses to resist evil persons on their own violent terms, was caught by Jesus' disciples and practiced in the apostolic communities after Pentecost. But the Gospels show us how difficult it was for them to really grasp this revolutionary new vision of love. They could not understand why Jesus did not organize and lead a violent uprising aimed at freeing God's people from the foreign oppressor.

Only with time did they come to realize that the full manifestation of God's redemptive love is found in the cross. The cross of Jesus was, in reality, the consequence of his nonresistant love for his enemies. The vicarious death of Jesus in behalf of the enemies of God lies at the very heart of the alternative to violence.

The New Testament would claim that this nonresistant, self-giving love whose clearest and highest expression was the cross of Jesus is, in fact, power for the oppressed. To confess that Jesus is Messiah (Christ) is to recognize that Jesus' particular style of life, his particular way of exercising power, is indeed God's way for his people, as well as his Messiah. To confess that Jesus Christ is Lord implies that Jesus' definition of power is, indeed, God's definition. It is the definition which will finally prevail, as the confessions of the messianic community indicate in, for example, Revelation 5:12, 13; 7:10-12; 12:10, 11.

We are so conditioned by fallen social structures that we invariably use society's concepts to express our own self-understanding as God's people. The meaning of power is a prime example of this problem. Paul dealt with the meaning of the term "power" in 1 Corinthians 1:17—2:5. In fallen society power is the ability to force others: by means of "signs" whereby others are forced to believe, by "wisdom" whose power overwhelms, or by the sword of the legionnaire capable of enforcing by means of threat (ultimately of death). But in kingdom values none of these are really power. Rather, the apparent weakness of self-giving, vulnerable love, whose highest expression is the cross of Jesus, is, in reality, the epitome of true power. It alone is ultimately able to really persuade.

Even while renouncing the violent exercise of power, Christians are often caught in the temptation to employ force in many subtle, or not so subtle, forms in the church as well as in the world. Inasmuch as Jesus is concretely the ultimate expression of power, all of these other veiled forms of force must be unmasked and rejected for the manifestations of human fallenness that they really are.

Throughout its history, and especially since the time of Constantine, the Christian church has given very little attention to the fundamental role of this radical love which should characterize God's people.

The church has given tremendous amounts of energy to develop confessions of faith to define essentials for belief. But in regard to the way we are specifically expected to imitate God himself, in indiscriminating, unselfish, and sacrificial love, the church in general has had very little to say. Small minorities of believers throughout history, however, have resisted the pressures of society and loved as God loves. Their example gives us fresh courage in our day.

The kingdom has come. In Jesus' teachings, he offers a series of pointers which reveal the basic character of the kingdom community which responds to God's intention for his people. Anger, unfaithfulness, falsehood, vengeance, and hatred in human relationships are all overcome in that community which is characterized by peace, respect for one another, mutual confidence, trustworthiness, sincerity, redemptive attitudes toward offenders, and unselfish love toward all, even those who are enemies. These are the fundamental features of the community of the kingdom, begun by the Messiah and anticipating the reign of God over the entire universe. One day it will appear in all of its splendor.

11.
Learning to Pray

The people of God celebrate a new reality in worship. In the life and death and resurrection of his Messiah, God has defeated the powers of evil which seem to control our world. God's worshiping people are, in fact, a sign that the new age has come in Jesus Christ.

Worship has always been an essential part of the agenda of God's people. Jesus assumed that his community would continue to worship through the same time-honored ways used by the Jews of his time: almsgiving (generous acts of mercy) (Mt. 6:2-4), prayer (5-15), and fasting (16-18). In this Jesus was more radical than innovative. He was more concerned that the spirituality of his disciples reflect the intention of God, than simply replacing the old forms with new ones. He insisted that all these practices conform to their real purpose in God's design.

Jesus begins his teaching on the spirituality of his people with a warning. The term translated "beware" (Mt. 6:1) is generally used in a negative sense in Matthew's Gospel. It is a serious matter when the practice of piety becomes separated from the totality of life under the sovereignty of God. In distinguishing between ethical and ritual obedience we tend to divide the life of the worshiper.

However, in the biblical tradition true worship is rooted in covenant relationships which include all parts of life (Micah

6:6-8). In Jesus' teaching spiritual relationships clearly have social dimensions and social matters are of spiritual importance. The biblical understanding of spirituality is global and resists all human attempts to set up categories which are exclusively religious.

The constant temptation of humanity is to forget that we live in relation to God. Therefore, all of life must constantly be submitted to the judgment of God. When we forget this need for God, we are liable to give too much importance to the judgment of other people. Our religious practices become mere "theater productions" put on in the presence of others. The Greek verb here translated "to be seen" (1) contains the root out of which the English word "theater" has evolved. Jesus says, in effect, that to seek the applause of others in our religious practices will finally deprive us of the only approval that really matters: God's. God does not share with us his right to exercise judgment. God has charged His community with the tasks of discernment and forgiveness of sins, but not judgment.

Jesus teaches that our relationship to God is essentially that of children to a loving parent. In this highly personal relationship, communication plays an important role. God wants to relate to us as persons, as sons and daughters. Therefore, praise, adoration, thanksgiving, confession, intercession, petition, and other expressions of our love for God are important. In this context the teaching of Jesus known as the "Lord's Prayer" serves as a model for our practice of prayer.

The Lord's Prayer (6:9-13) originally may have been a list of suggestions for the instruction of the disciples. The epistles of Paul and the Acts of the Apostles indicate that the Lord's Prayer was surely not the only legitimate form for prayer among Jesus' followers. Although the spirit of the Lord's Prayer was taken over by the New Testament community, the form of prayer in the gathered community was free and functional. In fact, prayer was living drama in the life of the messianic community (Acts 4:23-31).

There are six petitions in the Lord's Prayer. The first three have to do with God, and are therefore essentially praise or adoration. The last three refer to the basic needs of humankind, and are therefore supplication or petition. The Lord's

Prayer concentrates on that which is really essential to the life of the people of God. Therefore, reflection on these teachings will be instructive, not only for our understanding of prayer, but to understand life in the community of the Messiah.

1. "Our Father who art in heaven" (Mt. 6:9a)

To be able to address God as "Father," a loving and caring parent, constitutes the first and greatest element of prayer. Although it was common in Jewish prayers of the time to call on God as Father, the practice in the primitive Christian community surely owes its origin to Jesus. In the Synoptic Gospels Jesus refers to God as His Father in a highly significant way. (See, for example, Mt. 5:16; 48; 6:1, 4, 8, 14, 15; 7:11; 10:20, 29; 13:34; 18:14; 23:9.) The dominant motifs in these passages are: God is a parent who provides for his children with tender loving care, and he is the one who will judge them on the last day.

In other words, the Judge before whom we will stand on the final day is the same parent we already know through Jesus. God is the Father of Jesus, the Messiah. At the same time, he is the Father of those who participate in the messianic kingdom begun by Jesus.

In the early messianic community the invocation of God as "Father" showed a level of intimacy completely unknown among the Jews of the period. The point here was not to designate male or female but to show the family intimacy of a parent. It was a Jewish custom to substitute the term "heaven" for "God" in order to avoid pronouncing the divine name. In contrast, the apostolic church was accustomed to using the familiar Aramaic expression of intimate affection, "abba" (Gal. 4:6; Rom. 8:15; 14:36).

However, among the Jews abba was never applied to God. It was limited, instead, to the most intimate family relationships, such as that which little children might enjoy with their parents. Therefore, the modern equivalent of abba would probably be "daddy." Surely the disciples learned to use this term of familiar affection from Jesus himself. And to apply it to God was a courageous act in the socio-religious environment of first-century Judaism.

The whole Bible story
proved real in this one Go
what was best for them, an
to him they found life to be goc
talk to him and they could

2. "Hallowed be thy name" (Mt. 6:9b)

In effect, the messianic community is asking that the nature and intention of God be revealed and realized in the midst of humankind. God hallows his name in human history through the community which worships him.

In reality, the first petition anticipates and incorporates all those which follow: the coming of the kingdom, the fulfillment of God's will, the life of the messianic community, the need of bread, forgiveness, and liberation. All of these concerns are present, in essence, in the request that the "name" of God (his character, nature, and will) be revealed, recognized, reverenced, and obeyed among all people.

3. "Thy kingdom come" (Mt. 6:10a)

Another way of expressing this petition would be, "Bring in the kingdom which you have promised to us." Matthew uses the verb translated here "come" to designate both the historic coming of the Messiah in Jesus of Nazareth, as well as the second coming of Jesus in the awaited parousia. According to Matthew's Gospel, in the historic coming of Jesus the kingdom of God has drawn near in a definitive sense (Mt. 3:2; 10:7). This kingdom has been announced and persons are invited to enter it because Jesus has begun it in his person. And thanks

s of people whose faith was
They believed that he knew
whenever they were faithful
They found that they could
ear what he wanted them to do.
— Anna Mow

to the clear signs which Jesus has given to his followers, we can know the nature of this kingdom and confidently look forward to its fulfillment.

When Jesus' followers pray that the "kingdom come," they are not asking for some completely unknown and new thing. The kingdom of God is at hand in the person of Jesus and participation in this kingdom requires radical repentance (Mt. 4:17). The Sermon on the Mount furnishes a summary of the values in this kingdom.

Although Jesus has established this kingdom, it still awaits its full and final establishment at the end of human history. The people of God pray "thy kingdom come" because the kingdom of God is at one and the same time, a present reality and a future hope. This petition expresses concern for the fullest possible realization of this kingdom within human history, as well as its final coming in all of its glorious fullness.

4. "Thy will be done, on earth as it is in heaven" (Mt. 6:10b)

The will of God is to establish the kingdom in which the life revealed by Jesus is most fully realized. This petition expresses the hope that humankind will at last live up to God's

129

intention for it. This divine intention had been seen, sometimes dimly, in the law of the covenant. It had been glimpsed, sometimes faintly, in the proclamation of the prophets. Now Jesus was revealing it with crystal clarity. The messianic community prays for grace to obey the will of God, but its prayer is not limited to itself. It is concerned that the will of God be known and obeyed among all humankind, "on earth as it is in heaven."

In reality, this is a daring request. Only that community which is certain that it has received in Jesus Christ the definitive revelation of the will of God dares to pray in this way. This community is conscious that God's will has become a reality in the kingdom started by Jesus.

To pray in this way is to say, "May you soon be obeyed by all humanity in the same way in which you are obeyed in heaven." And this is not an exercise in theological fantasy to imagine how life in heaven will be. This prayer grows out of the clear conviction that the life of Jesus' kingdom is a faithful revelation of God's will in heaven.

5. "Give us this day our daily bread" (Mt. 6:11)

In this petition Jesus expresses concern for human life which is temporal and insecure. The first person plural pronouns (we, us, our) occur eight times in three verses (Mt. 6:11-13). They refer to the messianic community which grew up around Jesus and depends on the grace of God for its very life. This conviction has endured throughout the history of God's people.

Humankind truly depends on God to sustain its life, for its well-being, for its blessedness, and for its salvation. Yahweh is the one who "executes justice for the oppressed; who gives food to the hungry" (Ps. 146:7). The words "this day" in this petition underline the same idea of God's providence. Fragile creatures depend daily on the grace and providence of God. This dependence does not mean that people are therefore simply victims of circumstance from one day to another. The people of God know by experience that God is faithful "to all generations" and therefore they confront the future with confidence (Ps. 39:1).

The "bread" of this petition is material bread. It provides the nutrients necessary to sustain human life (Ps. 104:15). Before long in its history, the church began to give this "bread" a spiritual interpretation. The Christian church has generally found it relatively easy to trust in God for the salvation of the soul. But to really trust in God for survival in a hostile world has not come easily.

6. "And forgive us our debts, as we also have forgiven our debtors" (Mt. 6:12)

In the same way that we experience the forgiveness of God in the messianic community, so also our debts are mutually forgiven. In reality, this petition offers a description of the messianic community. Divine forgiveness is authentically experienced in that particular human community in which personal indebtedness, as well as offenses, are freely forgiven.

The Greek terms translated "debts" and "debtors" in this text carry the meaning of debt and debtor in a literal sense. Generally, their meaning in this text has been understood in religious terms, as offenses and offenders in a strictly spiritual sense. However, this language would seem to indicate that there is an especially close relationship in the messianic community between the mutual forgiveness of personal indebtedness and divine forgiveness. In Luke's version of the Lord's Prayer the meaning of this relationship appears even more clearly. "And forgive us our sins, for we ourselves forgive every one who is indebted to us" (Lk. 11:4). The present tense of the verb in the second phrase, "forgive," in reality implies that the people of God are accustomed to forgiving indebtedness.

Immediately following the Lord's Prayer, Matthew adds two verses (6:14, 15) in which Jesus offers additional comments about the meaning of this petition. Instead of using the term "debts," as he had done in verse 12, Jesus now uses "trespasses," or "offenses" (Mt. 6:14, 15). In this way Matthew makes the point that it is *also* necessary to forgive the offenses of other persons if we expect to really experience divine forgiveness for our offenses. In effect, what Jesus had said about "debts" (Mt. 6:12) also applies to offenses" (14, 15). Therefore, this passage really deals with two related questions: the forgiveness of indebtedness and the pardon of offenses.

7. "And lead us not into temptation, but deliver us from [the] evil [one]" (Mt. 6:13a)

The community gathered by the Messiah depends on the heavenly Father for its bread, forgiveness, and, finally, liberation. Our version of this passage, "lead us not into temptation," can give the impression that God is somehow responsible for temptations. But this implication is unfortunate. James 1:13, 14 declares clearly that God does not incite us to evil. The temptation to do wrong comes from another source. This petition expresses the community's hope that God will sustain them in the hour of testing.

The "temptation" mentioned in this petition is apparently some sort of diabolical attempt to turn God's people from their true purpose. The ultimate source of this temptation is the evil

Jan Gleysteen, photographer and Anabaptist lecturer from the Mennonite Publishing House in Pennsylvania.

one. Some versions of the New Testament translate this petition, "but save us from the evil one" (e.g., *The New English Bible* and *The Jerusalem Bible*).

The liberation of the messianic community is to be delivered from the control of the evil one and his "powers" which manifest themselves in so many different ways. The people of God live in the confidence that God will finally lead them into the "promised land" of the coming kingdom. Therefore, despite the community's engagement in constant conflict with evil in its many forms, they are sustained by hope, a hope which illumines the future based on God's faithfulness in the past and the present.

8. "For thine is the kingdom and the power and the glory, for ever. Amen." (Mt. 6:13b)

This doxology with which the Lord's Prayer ends does not appear in many of the more recent versions of the New Testament. It is not found in the oldest manuscripts. It is, however, representative of the kind of liturgical formula which expresses the firm conviction that the kingdom of the Messiah has within it the seeds of power and glory which will one day be revealed in all their fullness. Meanwhile the glorious form of the future kingdom is already prefigured in the experience of the messianic community.

This eschatological community (meaning that it already participates in the life of "the age to come") expresses its living hope through the doxologies with which it worships. This doxology is perfectly attuned to the spirit of the New Testament community so it should come as no surprise to find a number of similar doxologies in its pages (for example, Jude 25; Rev. 5:13; 11:15).

True Piety

Few aspects of the religious life bothered Jesus more than hypocrisy which led persons to pretend a piety. Worse yet, was the practice of piety to others for their approval, rather than to God, "the Father who sees in secret" (Mt. 6:4, 6, 18). For this reason Jesus charged the scribes and Pharisees with being "blind guides," "blind fools," "a child of hell," "whitewashed tombs" and "serpents" (Mt. 23).

But we should remember that hypocrisy is precisely the

temptation which most tantalizes religious people. The various forms with which we express our spiritual experiences are in the beginning generally authentic. They reflect the reality of our experience and obedience as members of the body of Christ. But in the absence of new and vital experiences in the life of the people of God the religious forms tend to become routine and eventually harden.

The history of the church warns us that with the passing of years, decades, and centuries we practice our piety for the purpose of keeping up appearances. And our practice of piety becomes a "theatrical production" because it no longer responds to the realities of fresh spiritual experience and continuing obedience.

The solution to this problem does not lie in religious innovation. It is not merely a matter of abandoning the expressions of our piety, our worship forms, in order to constantly begin anew. Jesus assumed that his disciples would continue these practices as concrete forms of expressing a relationship with God. But we need to be alert to the subtle dangers.

The remedy for the hypocritical show described in these passages is the continual cultivation of a fresh and authentic personal relationship with God. Under the searchlight of his judgment our practice of piety will be constantly renewed and we will continually experience new dimensions of relationship with God, as well as with our brothers and sisters in the family of God.

Conclusion

Worship is essential for the people of God. In its worship the community celebrates the new reality of the kingdom of God among them. Worship is based on a reconciled relationship with God and expresses itself in reconciling relationships with others. In this context, prayer is a vital ingredient of cosmic, as well as earthly, dimensions. Spontaneous praise and thanksgiving are evidences of real wholeness among God's people. Mutual understanding and forgiveness and generosity and sincerity are all characteristics of this worshiping community. Their personal relationship to the Father frees the people of God from practicing their spirituality for show or ostentation. They are freed to worship in spirit and truth.

12.
Seeking God's Kingdom Without Anxiety

The problem of property is not merely a question with economic, legal, or social issues. The context of Jesus' teachings on material goods clearly teaches that property is in reality, a spiritual issue which deeply affects our relationship with God. As with the practice of piety, so property influences all of our lives. The way material elements are acquired and used, as well as our inner attitudes toward them, are of fundamental importance in determining our relationship to God. In these teachings Jesus clearly proclaims the exclusive claim God makes on the life of his people.

Jesus' teachings in this rather complex section of the Sermon on the Mount can be organized around three specific instructions: (1) "Do not lay up for yourselves treasures on earth ... but lay up for yourselves treasures in heaven" (Mt. 6:19a, 20a). (2) "Do not be anxious about your life, what you shall eat or what you shall drink, nor about your body, what you shall put on.... Do not be anxious about tomorrow" (Mt. 6:25a, 31, 34a). (3) "But seek first his kingdom and his righteousness, and all these things shall be yours as well" (Mt. 6:33).

These instructions to God's people are presented in an imperative form and, as commands, they call for decision and appropriate action. The scope of the instructions themselves is broadened and their meaning is illustrated by means of a series of proverbs and popular sayings. These were typical in

Jewish literature of the period. Known as "wisdom" sayings, they stimulated the imagination of the hearers. They carried the listener to new levels of reflection and understanding and, at their best, to more obedient action.

"Do not lay up for yourselves treasures on earth where moth and rust consume and where thieves break in and steal, but lay up for yourselves treasures in heaven" (Mt. 6:19a, 20a).

The essentially perishable nature of material goods is depicted by the images of "moth," "rust," and "thieves." Garments which were hoarded at home ended up by being eaten by the larvae of moths. The coins and jewels which Palestinian peasants or laborers buried in the ground in periods of political and economic instability were sometimes completely disfigured by the wearing effects of the humidity and the soil. When they tried to save them by hiding them in their houses, thieves often stole them by making holes through the fragile mud bricks.

In contrast, "treasures in heaven" escape the destruction which "treasures on earth" are bound to suffer. But what are these "treasures in heaven"? And how are they laid up? The parallel passage in Luke sheds light on the meaning of this phrase: "Sell your possessions and give alms; provide yourselves . . . with a treasure in the heavens that does not fail, where no thief approaches and no moth destroys" (Lk. 12:33).

In other passages the phrase is understood in the same sense. Jesus, for example, said to the rich young ruler, "Sell what you possess and give to the poor, and you will have treasure in heaven" (Mt. 19:21; Mk. 10:21; Lk. 18:22). Regarding the rich fool, it was said, "So is he who lays up treasure for himself, and is not rich toward God" (Lk. 12:21). It appears that "treasures in heaven" are laid up by means of practicing generosity to the needy (see 1 Tim. 6:17-19). For Jesus, this insight must have been very important. Practically every time that he had something to say about riches or property he repeated these or similar words.

Jesus invites his disciples to be, in fact, a community of generosity. Those who have share with those who do not have what they need. In his call to repentance as preparation for the coming kingdom, John the Baptist had already caught the vision of this community nature of the new messianic order. "He who has two coats, let him share with him who has none; and he who has food, let him do likewise" (Lk. 3:11). Although Jesus does not give any concrete definitions about ways to implement this teaching, he does develop the principle with force and clarity.

One of the most pressing challenges which faces the Christian church of our time is, undoubtedly, the creation of concrete expressions of brotherhood in the sphere of economics. We need to find forms of living together and sharing which clearly express the principle which Jesus taught. The messianic community is not content to merely reproduce the economic models in our contemporary societies. Rather than merely attempting to humanize existing economic systems, God's people must dare to be extreme in giving concrete forms to the principles which Jesus taught.

To lend emphasis and clarity to the principle in the verses which follow, Jesus uses three phrases like the biblical proverbs:

1. "For where your treasure is, there will your heart be also" (Mt. 6:21). Originally "your," the possessive pronouns, are both in their singular form. Jesus often presented principles in general terms and than applied them personally and directly (by using the singular form) for the benefit of His disciples (Mt. 5:38-42). This verse reveals an important side of the biblical idea of person. The heart is attracted by the treasure freely chosen. Every person has a treasure. But no one can have more than one. The treasure which a person chooses in turn exercises exclusive power. Through this biblical proverb, Jesus warns us that the values which we choose for ourselves finally determine our destiny.

2. ". . . If your eye is sound, your whole body will be full of light; but if your eye is not sound, your whole body will be full of darkness" (Mt. 6:22b, 23a). According to Old Testament thought a person's eye is the lamp which guides one's life. If a person's eye is sound (literally, "single" or "good") this will be well accomplished. If, on the other hand, the eye is not sound (literally, "evil"), then the person will be lost in the darkness.

3. No one can serve two masters;
for either he will hate the one
and love the other,

Carolyn Charles Wenger, director of Lancaster Mennonite Historical Society in Pennsylvania.

or he will be devoted to the one
and despise the other.
You cannot serve God and mammon.—Matthew 6:24

These words in context show the radical character of Jesus' teachings in relation to riches and property. Material possessions become a false god who demand the same loyalty from persons that God requires. For this reason the demands which material possessions impose upon a person must be rejected outright.

Based on its form, this verse appears to be a Hebrew proverb in which the main idea is spoken in the first line and is developed and deepened in successive lines. In this way Jesus emphasizes what he has already said about fundamental human nature: persons will always place themselves and their services at the disposal of someone or something. To imagine that one is totally free and therefore servant to no one appears to be utterly pretentious. To imagine that one can serve two masters is to fool oneself.

The term "to belong to" probably offers a better translation of the biblical idea of service reflected in verse 24. It is not merely a matter of giving some service, but rather the kind of total availability which a master could expect of his slave. This verse reflects the kind of relationship which excludes all other loyalties. To "hate" (line 2) means to separate oneself in total indifference from someone. To "love" in this context carries the opposite meaning. It means to belong to another, and to serve that person with one's whole being. To "be devoted to" (line 3) translates a term which means to attach oneself to another; and to "despise" means the opposite, to separate oneself from another.

In the last line of verse 24 Jesus offers a brief and powerful summary of his teaching on this subject. A person serves God by means of concrete expressions of unselfish and self-giving love toward others. And this, by the nature of things, is the way in which a person lays up treasures in heaven. On the other hand, a person serves mammon by centering one's life and affections around material values. Jesus calls this way of living "laying up treasures on earth." Mammon is the Aramaic term for "profits." Therefore some English versions use the term "money." Mammon is used especially as having an evil power such as that which is used by a false god.

In this teaching Jesus is not denying the validity of material goods which are so necessary to support human life. However, his words do cut deeply and place before us a bewildering dilemma. To what degree is it possible for us to possess properties and money without allowing ourselves to fall into their possession? The people of God are called to find ways to resist the temptation to "love" them, to "be devoted" to them, to "serve" them.

"Do not be anxious about your life, what you shall eat or what you shall drink, nor about your body, what you shall put on. . . . Do not be anxious about tomorrow" (Mt. 6:25a, 31, 34a).

Here again Jesus identifies a principle: it does not make sense to be anxious about one's life in the messianic community (Mt. 6:25a). In the following verses he describes more fully what he means by this anxiety about life. It includes the question of food, drink, clothing, and a secure future. Here too this principle is clarified, illustrated, and broadened by another series of Hebrew proverbs and popular wisdom sayings.

Six times in these ten verses (Mt. 6:25-34) Jesus repeats a term which is translated in our version by the phrase "be anxious." Jesus is here referring to that kind of anxiety which leads to a divided loyalty and then to an idolatrous emphasis on material possessions.

The New Testament recognizes that human existence is characterized by struggle and concern. The many warnings against being anxious begin with human nature: that everybody tends to be anxious in one way or another. God's people will engage in productive work like other persons. But they will do so free of worry and anxiety because as persons who already belong to God's kingdom, and its values help determine all that happens in their lives. So their "concerns" will not exceed what is necessary in order to provide for the needs of their brothers and sisters, as well as their own (Eph. 4:28).

Anxiety is, in reality, a pagan characteristic (Mt. 6:7, 32). Anxious people do not realize that there is a "Father who knows what you need" (Mt. 6:8). In the messianic community the uncertainties of life do not cause anxiety because its members know, by experience and faith, that the future and the present are in God's hands. Jesus' remedy for anxiety is confidence in God in the context of the community of the kingdom. Jesus underscores this confidence with four illustrations:

1. "Is not life more than food, and the body more than clothing?" (Mt. 6:25b). Because God's children, who have been created in his image as living beings, are worth infinitely more than the food which sustains them and the clothing which covers their bodies, we may confidently trust in the providence of God to keep and protect those whom he has created. God can be counted on to care about our food and clothing, since he, after all, concerns himself about our very lives.

2. "Look at the birds of the air . . . the lilies of the field . . . the grass of the field" (Mt. 6:26, 28, 30). Of course birds struggle for their survival. But in and of themselves they would be incapable of providing for themselves. But God provides for them far beyond their own efforts. The purpose of this illustration is to show that if God looks after birds, and indeed he does, how much more will he care for humans. And if the Creator crowns with so much beauty the flowers and the grass of the fields which flourish for only a day, he can surely be counted on to look after his children in the human family.

3. "And which of you by being anxious can add one cubit to his span of life?" (Mt. 6:27). Human anxieties, and even those concerns which might be considered to be legitimate, show us that there are unsurmountable limits to what we are capable of attaining. God alone is able to cause the body to grow taller or one's life span to be extended. In the face of these limitations human anxiety seems all the more foolish. The accumulation of material possessions will not even serve to prolong the life of the anxious possessor one "cubit" more.

4. "Let the day's own trouble be sufficient for the day" (Mt. 6:34). Confident trust in God, as Father, and an all-consuming search for the kingdom free one from the anxieties of an unknown future. Furthermore, in the face of today's troubles, it is doubly foolish to waste time and energies worrying about tomorrow.

Of course, our economic structures are different from the ones in first-century Palestine. Has what we call "insurance" and "savings" hidden from us the meaning of what Jesus called an anxious concern for tomorrow? Is the usury which was forbidden in the Gospels now considered legitimate when called "charging interest"? Undoubtedly the nature of wealth and inflation has changed our situation. Nevertheless, Jesus has here offered some principles which we dare not disregard without grave risk to our spiritual well-being. When savings accumulate, investments grow unreasonably, and interest charges become an excessive burden for a brother in need, then these warnings of Jesus must be taken seriously.

"But seek first his kingdom and his righteousness, and all these things shall be yours as well" (Mt. 6:33).

In this instruction Jesus summarizes his teaching about property, material possessions, and money. Anxiety grows out of a scale of values which is really pagan in its essence. People who try to assure their future only by means of accumulating material possessions are, in reality, condemning themselves to an anxious existence. On the other hand, followers of Jesus have an all-consuming cause to which they are dedicated—the kingdom of God and his righteousness.

The solution to the oppressive pagan anxiety which characterizes people in our time is found in the messianic community. The person who seeks security in property, in possessions and fiscal solvency stands condemned to a life of anxiety. But the one who seeks the kingdom of God finds freedom from anxieties, for God's grace both sustains that life and provides all a person's needs.

Clearly, from this summary statement, Jesus is not proposing the passive and resigned trust in providence which has sometimes characterized Oriental thought and practice. Neither does he suggest a sort of mystical contempt for the physical body and its needs in contrast to the soul and a person's spiritual needs. Nor does he teach a naive optimism which refuses to take seriously the harsh realities of human existence on this earth. Instead, he calls on persons to look for that which is of real value, "the kingdom of God and his righteousness."

The righteousness of the kingdom is God's gift which makes it possible for persons to live together in harmonious and just relationships. For the people of God a personally satisfying simple life becomes possible. Material goods are

Christ has taught us how to love,
in the midst of conflict.
His Holy Spirit is among us to guide us
and heal our brokenness.
And he has promised us grace
to overcome the world.

—Anna Juhnke

administered in line with God's purposes and there are resources to provide for those in need. The absolute loyalty of this community to God frees its members from the anxieties of an oppressive materialistic orientation. Among God's people life is shared in the spirit of Jesus Christ.

The understanding of the place of material goods in human society is basic and revolutionary. We tend to think of ourselves and our own needs first and then to think of others. Jesus asks the opposite of his followers. He invites persons to enter God's family which already has the nature of the kingdom which will one day be revealed in all its splendor. Here no one lives for self alone. Here life is shared and provision is made for all of a person's needs. Here the Father who works through his generous community cares for all.

In reality, this is the same spirit which we find reflected in the primitive community in Jerusalem (Acts 2:43-47; 4:32-37) and in the various Christian communities to which Paul's letters were directed (Rom. 12:13; Eph. 4:28), as well as John's (1 Jn. 3:16-18) and James's (2:15-17). Throughout the later history of the church this spirit has manifested itself many times. The economic practices of the community have taken on fraternal dimensions whenever men and women have been touched anew by the living Spirit of God and have taken seriously these teachings of Jesus.

The Christian church (surely by no mere oversight) has tended to play down the real meaning of these teachings. Although Jesus said that it would be extremely difficult for a rich person to enter the kingdom of heaven, the church has generally gone out of its way to make it easy. Some churches even congratulate themselves for the rich and the powerful who appear on their membership roles. Jesus and the apostles warned of the grave dangers which property and wealth bring to the people of God. Many churches, on the other hand, have attempted to enhance their position in society by strengthening their economic and institutional base, either through their own financial holdings or through wealthy members. In fact, some professing Christians have considered financial solvency and economic power to be signs of God's pleasure and rewards for virtue rather than dangers and sources of temptation.

The Christian churches have treated Jesus' parallel teachings concerning vengeance and violence in a similar way. The full impact of Jesus' instructions has been softened so that only "legitimate" vengeance is exacted and only "justifiable" violence is employed. In fact the church has often bought its security by using secular power rather than taking the hazardous path of peacemaking and self-giving love. Christians have generally felt justified in defending their rights through the violence of self-defense and legal action instead of opting for the vulnerability which Jesus practiced and taught to his disciples. In fact, many Christians consider the use of violence in the interests of so-called "just" causes to be a virtue.

However, we need to take both of these teachings with equal seriousness. In reality, both carry the stamp of Jesus' own authority. Both nonresistance and detachment from material possessions, when put into practice, require the grace and providence of God for survival. Sharing goods, as well as renouncing all recourse to violence in social relationships, are humanly hazardous steps. They show a confident trust in God in a violent and materialistic society.

Conclusion

The people of God dare to trust in God for both their life and their survival. Contrary to all other human societies, the messianic community refuses to be "anxious" about its future. This community is freed from false loyalties to other pretenders and serves God with undivided devotion. Freed from fears for the present and the future and freed from the idolatrous tyranny of mammon, the people of God are the salt of the earth and light for the world.

13.
Bearing Fruit

The community described in the Sermon on the Mount is not a utopia, a beautiful vision which is never realized. It is a family of men and women who respond to the Messiah's invitation to experience, by the grace of God, the life which corresponds to the kingdom.

Nevertheless, in relation to the rest of human society the people of God are forced to live against the current. We can best understand Jesus' teachings in the last chapter of the Sermon on the Mount in this context. In order to protect the people of God from the dangers and in order to conserve the different quality of their life in his community, Jesus offers a series of instructions and warnings. These instructions are related to the problems and dangers which confront the community and threaten their very life.

1. "Judge not" (Mt. 7:1-5). This instruction notes the way in which spiritual discernment and forgiveness are carried out among the people of God. It is summarized in its most concise form in the counsel: "Judge not, that you be not judged" (Mt. 7:1). Here Jesus is dealing with the problem which occurs in a community whose moral standards are high. The ethical zeal of its members can easily lead to attitudes of moral and spiritual superiority. Motivated by what they erroneously believe to be a high degree of responsibility before God and other believers, these persons begin to criticize, to pass judg-

ment, and even to condemn their brothers and sisters for their faults.

Sometimes the counsel "judge not" has been taken in an absolute sense, to prohibit all intervention in others' problems. This interpretation overlooks the teaching in verse 5 with which Jesus concludes this particular instruction. Jesus does not intend to forbid expressions of mutual concern within the community. He does, however, insist that the purpose of discipline is to restore. The verb translated "judge" does not mean merely to form an opinion or evaluation about the brother or sister's action. It means, rather, to pass judgments or to condemn. The parallel passage in Luke's Gospel makes this meaning of the verse clear (Lk. 6:37).

Matthew 7:3-5 underscores the importance of exercising mutual discipline in the messianic community, but we are warned of possible deformations in the process. We dare not condemn our brothers and sisters, but restore them in a spirit of true humility. The example of the "speck" and the "log" suggest that only a person who has experienced repentance and forgiveness (from whose eye a log has been removed) is in condition to help a sister and brother with their problem (remove the speck from their eye). In order to live up to our best intentions as disciples of Jesus, we need the help of our brothers and sisters. Our defensive mechanisms do not even allow us to see our own defects, let alone to correct them.

The path to restoration and forgiveness is always personal and requires a spirit of genuine humility. The reconciliation of an erring brother or sister requires that someone in the community show concern for them. The removal of a "speck" from someone else's eye is a very delicate procedure and requires an abundance of tender loving care.

2. "Ask . . . seek . . . knock" (Mt. 7:7-11). At first impression, this instruction appears to be a continuation of Jesus' earlier teaching on prayer (Mt. 6:5-15). However, according to verse 11, the conclusion, the emphasis does not fall so much on the practice of prayer as it does on the fact that "even more will your Father who is in heaven give *good things* to those who ask him!" In Luke's version, Jesus declares exactly what this "good thing" is: "How much more will the heavenly Father give the *Holy Spirit* to those who ask him" (11:13)!

147

To live a life based on the Sermon on the Mount requires infinitely more than the best of human efforts. In order to live the life of the kingdom, the Spirit of the Lord of the kingdom is needed. Through the Spirit, God himself enters into the new messianic era begun by Jesus, to enable and to purify those who participate in his kingdom.

We cannot honestly read the Sermon on the Mount without feeling humanly powerless and thoroughly prostrated by its requirements. Purely human resources are totally inadequate in the face of its demands. To this sense of human incapacity and frustration Jesus responds, "Ask . . . seek . . . knock" (Mt. 7:7), and the Father will give you his Spirit. This is precisely the prophetic vision of the messianic era. "A new heart I will give you, and a new spirit I will put within you. . . . And I will put my Spirit within you, and cause you to talk in my statutes and be careful to observe my ordinances" (Ezek. 36:26, 27). The life of God's people is not merely a question of understanding the will of God and keeping his commandments. It is also communion in the Holy Spirit who makes all of this possible.

3. "Do so to them" (Mt. 7:12). The plural form of the "golden rule" ("you" in this verse is plural) indicates that the point of reference is not the self-centered individual, but rather the messianic community in which persons seek the well-being of others. The golden rule in reality serves to broaden the scope of the Sermon on the Mount. In the Sermon on the Mount Jesus did not really intend to touch every situation which arises in the life of his disciples. But it is sufficiently inclusive and specific to describe with clarity the form and direction which the life of the Christian community will take. The golden rule offers a principle which covers situations which are not specifically dealt with in the Sermon on the Mount.

This verse does not teach us that we should do good to others in order that they will return kindness to us. On the contrary, we are called upon to do for others what we would desire for ourselves. The motivation behind our behavior lies within the person who acts, and not in the form in which other persons may respond.

To order one's relationships according to the golden rule is to fulfill "the law and the prophets." In effect, this is a fuller expression of God's intention already revealed in the Old

It would not be so hard to believe if it were not so hard to obey.

Soren Kierkegaard

Testament. By ordering their actions according to the golden rule, Jesus' disciples move toward the fullest intention of God for his people. Of course, this leads to action which is fully consistent with the great commandment and its complement, "You shall love the Lord your God with all your heart, and with all your soul, and with all your mind.... And ... You shall love your neighbor as yourself" (Mt. 22:37, 39).

4. "Enter by the narrow gate" (Mt. 7:13, 14). This warning is related to the alternative offered by the "wide gate" and the "easy way." Apparently these are persons outside the community of Jesus whose way of life seems to be as acceptable as it is comfortable. This easy life, together with its corresponding values, presents a temptation to many Christians.

What generally goes unnoticed behind the facade of apparent happiness are the problems which cause worry and the dreams which escape fulfillment. On closer look we see greed which separates and deep loneliness which crowds cannot help, and, finally, self-destruction.

On the other hand, the life described in the Sermon on the Mount needs to be lived against the stream. The system of values of the messianic community is fundamentally opposed to the "easy way." Note, for example, the attitudes in relation to wealth and the exercise of power, the role of truthfulness, the importance of fidelity, and the attitude toward wrongdoers. Although we live in the kingdom by God's grace, our lives call for self-discipline and accepting mutual responsibility for discipleship.

Here Jesus is not describing a long road to travel, at the end of which we will finally obtain salvation. In reality, salvation is not considered apart from life in the kingdom of the Messiah. These verses define Jesus' call for decision, to enter into life, to enter into the kingdom. And having passed through the "narrow gate," one has already arrived at the goal in a very real sense. Life in the messianic community as described in the Sermon on the Mount is the form of the salvation God gives to his people. And in it we see a fleeting but true glimpse of the form it will take when the kingdom comes in all its fullness.

5. "Beware of false prophets" (Mt. 7:15-20). False prophets arise within the Christian community. More often than not, they can scarcely be distinguished from true disciples. In fact, on

the surface they seem to be authentic sheep. But eventually the results of their activity betray them and show them for what they really are.

In Matthew 7:16-20 the images change to that of a tree and its fruits. In this context the "fruits" undoubtedly refer to the concrete conduct which characterized the false prophets. But they may also refer to the moral character of the followers which these false prophets gathered around themselves. In other words, the authenticity or falseness of prophets will be recognized by the moral life of the communities which emerge in response to their teachings. We are told twice (Mt. 7:16, 20) that the character of the Christian prophet can be judged by the kind of fruits produced. The followers, as well as the ethical life of the authentic prophet, will reflect the values described in the Sermon on the Mount. In the false prophets this messianic ethic will not be observed.

Matthew 7:16-19 takes for granted an idea which our modern mentality finds strange. In reality, persons (in this case prophets) *are* what they *do,* and not what they profess to be or what they say. If they produce good fruit, they are a good tree. If they give bad fruit, they are a bad tree. It is simply impossible for a good tree to produce bad fruit or a bad tree to give good fruit. The possibility of making a distinction between the fundamental character of a person on one hand, and what that person does on the other hand, shows a modern dualistic understanding of persons. According to the vision presented here, it is impossible to separate between the ethical life of persons and their fundamental character.

6. "Lord, Lord" (Mt. 7:21-23). This warning is directed toward false brothers and sisters within the community. In these verses, clearly Jesus expects his disciples to give unconditional obedience to the will of God. And this will of God is known by all, because it has been revealed by Jesus through his life and teachings. Apparently these false prophets were persons in the community who displayed the capacity to transmit messages from God, do exorcisms, work other miracles, as well as practicing a seemingly exemplary piety. However, their lives were not clear human expressions of the Sermon on the Mount.

But no spiritual accomplishment can make up for the

absence of a style of life consistent with the example and the teachings of Jesus. Without an ethical life which, in reality, reflects Jesus' way of being and doing, it is useless to pretend that we are the community of the Messiah. Our good intentions, our valid social concerns, our visions for reform, our church or institutional achievements, our startling messages, and our attention-getting miracles will not suffice.

The phrase "not every one who says to me, Lord, Lord" (Mt. 7:21) refers to a situation in which true discipleship is turned into something easier and more attractive. Apparently these disciples' practice of spirituality attracts attention. The name of the Lord is constantly on their lips. (The present tense of "says" indicates a practice which has become customary.) In fact they rely on pronouncing the "name" to execute their remarkable miracles (Mt. 7:22). But Jesus declares that this spirituality is in reality an obvious deception. These persons really do not, nor will they, participate in the kingdom of heaven. Authentic participation in the kingdom is limited to those who do "the will of my Father" (Mt. 7:21).

"Many" (Mt. 7:22) is frequently used in Matthew's Gospel to describe those upon whom the judgment of God will come (Mt. 7:13; 19:30; 22:14). Here it applies to followers whose dedication to spiritual activism has detracted them from the most basic demands of the kingdom. Apparently even exercising charismatic gifts (prophesy, exorcisms, and mighty works done in the name of Jesus) is capable of turning many Christians aside from their fundamental relationships with brothers and sisters, or from their neighbors. Paul also found it necessary to warn that these gifts are vain without love (1 Cor. 13:2). Those who do not practice the values of the kingdom— in spite of expressions of spirituality—are not now, nor will they be on the final day, recognized by their Lord.

The term translated "evil" (Mt. 7:23) means literally lawlessness or the absence of law. The evil of these false disciples consists in not listening to their Lord; in disobeying the purpose of God, as declared in the teachings of Jesus. The will of God is the "new law" as declared with authority by the Messiah, the "new Moses."

7. "Every one then who hears these words of mine and does them ..." (Mt. 7:24-27). Jesus directs the warning of

Reba Place Fellowship, a Brethren and Mennonite church community in Evanston, Illinois.

these verses toward those who do not put into practice the new law of the kingdom which he has given in the Sermon on the Mount. The parable of the two houses makes it clear that Jesus intended that the teachings included in the Sermon on the Mount should be obeyed. The new law of the kingdom has been announced for all who have begun to experience the joy of the messianic age—the Beatitudes. To pretend to be citizens of the Messiah's new world without putting into practice Jesus' teachings is utter folly. The total ruin of those who do not practice Jesus' instructions is announced.

The phrase "every one then who hears these words of mine and does them" (Mt. 7:24) refers to the followers of Jesus who have responded enthusiastically and have begun to put into practice his teachings. The "wise man" (Mt. 7:24) is not merely an expression which describes the quality of a person's soul or spirit. Here the term refers to a person's concrete ethical behavior. The wise person is one who knows what should be done and does it.

In the biblical tradition to be wise, or prudent, is to believe and to obey. It implies both hearing and doing. In effect, Jesus tells us that persons construct their lives by putting into practice what they have heard, just as one builds a house by carrying out the plan. To build "upon a rock" in this case is to put into practice "these words" of Jesus (Mt. 7:24).

In this case, the torrential rains, together with the flooding which they produce, as well as the hurricane-like winds are simply proofs that the house is well built (Mt. 7:25). The firmness of the person who puts Jesus' words to practice will be demonstrated in an incident of testing.

On the other hand, the "foolish man" does not put into practice these words of Jesus (Mt. 7:26). The folly of the "foolish man" does not consist in his not listening to the words of Jesus, nor in his not having perceived their importance. In fact, the context seems to indicate that he delighted himself in them spiritually. His madness lies in his having heard them without doing them.

In the light of Christian church history this parable calls us to serious reflection. The Beatitudes with which Jesus described the essential character of those who participate in the kingdom have had a limited impact on the life of the church as a whole. The thoroughgoing new dimensions which Jesus gave to the ancient law of God have gone largely unnoticed in the church's practice. They have generally found expression only within marginal groups in Christendom.

Anger in interpersonal relationships, infidelity in marital relationships, falsehood in social relationships, vengeance toward the offender, and hatred of one's enemies are left behind when an ethic of self-giving love is released to respond to God's real intention for human life together. But such newness has found little echo in the institutional church.

For the vast majority of Christians, Jesus' teachings represent a goal which is altogether unrealistic. Therefore, we regulate marital problems by means of divorce, limit falsehood through the swearing of oaths to be truthful, limit vengeance by legal restrictions on retaliation, and keep violence from getting entirely out of control by a doctrine of legitimate self-defense and the just war. This level of morality is the expectation of most modern Christians.

Jesus warns against hypocrisy in the practice of our spirituality, but religiosity, unaccompanied by a corresponding growth in serious ethical commitment, is on the increase in the church. Jesus warned against the anxious laying up of "treasures on earth." Yet Christians in the Northern and Western hemispheres (where traditional Christianity is largely to be found) continue to enrich themselves at the expense of the poor and hungry of the world.

Jesus warned against those merely spiritualistic expressions of faith which are unconcerned about the fundamental question of social justice and self-giving love. Jesus warned against the folly of indulging oneself in the spiritual delights of religious language without the accompanying practice of obedience. But, where are those who are willing to build the "house upon the rock"?

Epilogue

The biblical story is the story of a people—the people of God. By God's grace fallen humanity was offered a community of salvation which bears God's name, reflects his nature, lives by his values, and proclaims his glory. The human predicament is recorded since the dawn of salvation history. It is reflected from the very beginning in the violence of Cain against his brother; in humankind's misguided attempt at Babel to establish its identity and secure its future in a group of its own making; in the bondage of Egypt which at its best offered fish and melons with leeks and onions.

Fallenness is reflected in a false trust in the monarchy which made Israel "like the nations" and in the oppressive cultic establishment of first-century Judaism accompanied by the heavy yoke of rabbinic pharisaism. Fallenness has followed the church throughout its history when it has institutionalized the salvation it offers.

But in all these humanly hopeless situations God has manifested his saving grace. God placed his mark of grace on the offender, and even in his judgment he showed mercy. God's alternative to the futility of Babel was the call of Abraham—the formation of a people who would live by faith. God's answer to Egyptian bondage was the redemption of the Exodus. A people was reconstituted by the gracious provisions of his covenant. God's word to Israel in the face of the moral bankruptcy of both civil and religious establishments was hope beyond judgment—the new community of the Messiah.

In the fullness of time God's answer to a people living under a yoke too heavy to bear is his Messiah—the true vine of God's own planting. Jesus begins the new community in which the eternal values of the kingdom prevail, thanks to the power of the Spirit of God in their midst. And thanks to the living presence of the Spirit and the Word in the midst of God's people, movements of authentic renewal have branched out again and again. Freeing themselves from the enslaving effects of social and religious institutionalism, these movements have become once more God's community of the Spirit.

The values by which God's people live reflect his nature and have been revealed most clearly by his Messiah.

God's people are characterized by a spirit of humility.

They are deeply concerned for the social and spiritual well-being of others.

They are nonresistant.

They are moved to action by their concern for justice.

They are characterized by a spirit of forgiveness, generosity, sincerity, and peace.

Anger, unfaithfulness, falsehood, vengeance, and hatred in relationships are all overcome in the messianic community.

Their community is characterized by peace, respect for one another, mutual confidence, trustworthiness, sincerity, redemptive attitudes toward offenders, and self-giving love toward all, even those who are enemies.

Their personal relationship with God frees them from the temptation to practice their piety for reasons of ostentation.

They are sustained by sincere confidence in their "heavenly Father" who cares for them.

They are nurtured by prayer and praise.

The community of the Messiah is empowered by the Holy Spirit.

God's people are those who love one another even as Christ, who laid down his life for his friends (and his enemies), has loved them. This is the only human community whose members, by definition, are bound to lay down their very lives for others. THESE ARE GOD'S COMMUNITY.

Bibliography

Suggestions for further reading

General

Burkholder, J. R. and Redekop, Calvin (editors). **Kingdom, Cross, and Community.** Scottdale: Herald Press, 1976.

Gish, Arthur **Living in Christian Community.** Scottdale: Herald Press, 1979.

Chapters 1-5

Bender, Harold S. **These Are My People: The Nature of the Church and Its Discipleship According to the New Testament.** Scottdale: Herald Press, 1962.

Brueggemann, Walter. **The Land.** Philadelphia: Fortress Press, 1977.

de Dietrich, Suzanne, **The Witnessing Community.** Philadelphia: The Westminster Press, 1958.

Kraus, C. Norman. **The Community of the Spirit.** Grand Rapids: William B. Eerdmans Publishing Company, 1974.

_____. **The Authentic Witness.** Grand Rapids: William B. Eerdmans Publishing Company, 1979.

Lind, Millard C. "Reflections on Biblical Hermeneutics," **Kingdom, Cross, and Community,** editors J. R. Burkholder and Calvin Redekop. Scottdale: Herald Press, 1976.

Minear, Paul. **Images of the Church in the New Testament.** Philadelphia: The Westminster Press, 1960.

Swartley, Willard M. **Mark: The Way for All Nations,** Scott-
dale: Herald Press, 1979.
Yoder, John H. **The Original Revolution.** Scottdale: Herald
Press, 1971.
_____. **The Politics of Jesus.** Grand Rapids: William B.
Eerdmans Publishing Company, 1972.

Chapters 6-7

Bauman, Harold E. "Forms of Covenant Community,"
Kingdom, Cross, and Community, editors J. R.
Burkholder and Calvin Redekop, Scottdale:
Herald Press, 1976.
Brown, Dale W. "The Free Church of the Future," **Kingdom,
Cross, and Community,** editors J. R. Burkholder
and Calvin Redekop, Scottdale: Herald Press,
1976.
Durnbaugh, Donald F. **The Believers' Church: The History
and Character of Radical Protestantism.** New
York: Macmillan, 1968.
Dyck, Cornelius J. (editor). **An Introduction to Mennonite
History.** Scottdale: Herald Press, 1967.
Klaassen, Walter. **Anabaptism: Neither Catholic nor
Protestant.** Waterloo: Conrad Press, 1973.

Chapters 8-13

Davies, W. D. **The Sermon on the Mount.** Cambridge: The
Cambridge University Press, 1966.
Driver, John. **Community and Commitment.** Scottdale:
Herald Press, 1976.
Hunter, Archibald M. **A Pattern for Life: An Exposition of the
Sermon on the Mount** (Revised Edition).
Philadelphia: The Westminster Press, 1965.
Jordan, Clarence. **Sermon on the Mount** (Revised Edition).
Valley Forge: Judson Press, 1970.
Kraybill, Donald B. **The Upside-Down Kingdom.** Scottdale:
Herald Press, 1978.
Miller, John W. **The Christian Way.** Scottdale: Herald Press,
1969.
Ramseyer, Robert L. (editor). **Mission and the Peace Wit-
ness.** Scottdale: Herald Press, 1979.
Sider, Ronald J. **Christ and Violence.** Scottdale: Herald
Press, 1979.